D1622487

Praise for *Category Creation*

"It has been a pleasure to partner with Gainsight since its earliest days in driving the creation of Customer Success as a true function in SaaS. Having been a category creator myself, I know it is a different journey, especially in the first years. The standard 'disruptor' playbook just doesn't work as well. Anthony's incredible tome does just that, for the first time in enterprise software. It gives you the playbook to creating, rather than reinventing, a category."

—Jason Lemkin, VC and Founder, SaaStr

"Customers create categories—not companies. *Category Creation* gives entrepreneurs and marketers from companies of all sizes and industries a blueprint for how to engage customers to validate, shape, and advance the interests of their market."

**—Jill Rowley, Partner, Stage 2 Capital,
and former Chief Growth Officer, Marketo**

"In the hierarchy of powers that determines the value of a company, category power is the highest, and if you are the company that creates and leads a new category, that is as good as it gets ever. *Category Creation* is a game plan for doing just that."

—Geoffrey A. Moore, Author, *Crossing the Chasm* and *Zone to Win*

"The ability to create a new category is not unique to startups. The largest companies in the world can play their advantages to build new markets and develop leadership positions within them. The tactics that Anthony lays out in *Category Creation* are just as relevant for today's Fortune 100 companies as they are for earlier stage businesses."

—Lori Wright, General Manager, Office, Microsoft

"We've reached a new era of software where companies are moving from IT stacks to cloud ecosystems—presenting today's entrepreneurs with a unique opportunity to create net new categories of products that reinvent complex processes of the past with simple solutions for the digital age. Gainsight is a great modern success story for this emerging business strategy. I'm excited to see Anthony share his playbook with the industry."

—Aaron Levie, CEO, Box

"We are in the midst of a digital gold rush, as companies of all sizes are recognizing new market opportunities and creating movements behind those causes for their brands. I'm thrilled to see Anthony put pen to paper to demystify category creation and help other executives follow the lead of market makers like Gainsight and others."

—Sue Barsamian, former Chief Sales and Marketing Officer, Hewlett-Packard Enterprise Software

"It always surprises me that category creation isn't better understood and more enthusiastically embraced by business leaders. I've had the privilege of being a part of four great companies—GMF Robotics, Rasna, Ariba, and DocuSign—and every time, category creation was a key to our success. Anthony has been a student of this innovative business approach and, in *Category Creation*, invites other leaders to activate their courage to challenge the status quo."

—Keith Krach, Chairman and CEO, Ariba and DocuSign

Categ●ry Creati●n

Categ●ry Creati●n

HOW TO BUILD A BRAND THAT **CUSTOMERS, EMPLOYEES,** AND **INVESTORS WILL LOVE**

ANTHONY KENNADA

WILEY

Published by John Wiley & Sons, Inc., Hoboken, New Jersey.

Published simultaneously in Canada.

For general information on our other products and services or for technical support, please contact our Customer Care Department within the United States at (800) 762–2974, outside the United States at (317) 572–3993 or fax (317) 572–4002.

Wiley publishes in a variety of print and electronic formats and by print-on-demand. Some material included with standard print versions of this book may not be included in e-books or in print-on-demand. If this book refers to media such as a CD or DVD that is not included in the version you purchased, you may download this material at http://booksupport.wiley.com. For more information about Wiley products, visit www.wiley.com.

Library of Congress Cataloging-in-Publication Data:
ISBN 9781119611561 (Hardcover)
ISBN 9781119611585 (ePDF)
ISBN 9781119611615 (ePub)

Cover design: Wiley

Printed in the United States of America
V10013384_082719

To Nick Mehta and the Gainsight marketing team—past, present, and future—whose "crambition" launched a movement and inspired a new playbook for human first marketing. You are the co-authors of this story.

Contents

Foreword

When I first picked up the draft of *Category Creation* that Anthony Kennada shared with me, I had that feeling one sometimes gets at high school or college reunions—one memory after another that brings back old associations, celebrations at bold decisions and fortuitous timing, and the occasional cringe at a misstep or dead-end path. And, for sure, Anthony's joy at recounting the heady days of starting not just a company, but a full-on movement, is a familiar reminisce for others who have been there, who were "there at the beginning" of their own category creation moment.

But, far from a mere collection of boorish stories from the glory days, each chapter I read offered a fresh take—either a codified playbook for startup entrepreneurs on what once used to be an unscientific mix of instinct, personality, connections, and some smarts; or an ongoing call to action for leaders of established companies who perhaps have already created a category, or who suspect there is a way to leverage and break out of the category they've been in for years. In our early days at HubSpot, we sensed that there was a parade that we could get in front of, that we had happened upon an unfolding shift in buyer behavior among businesspeople that mirrored what was already somewhat apparent in consumer behavior. Fortunately for us, the playbook we came up with was a direct reflection of the movement we were advocating: Inbound Marketing. The best way to tell the story of inbound marketing was to excel at inbound marketing. The playbook and the newly created category were actually the same thing.

The playbook Anthony lays out doesn't need to be discovered through alchemy and luck. Much of what he shares are elements that are common sense in some ways, but counterintuitive in others. Even after more than ten years later in our own category at HubSpot, we find there continues to be great value in making these factors explicit, and finding ways to measure them.

Human-centric. At HubSpot, we say "Grow Better" and mean very much what Anthony observes when he says that "category creation seeks to reinforce a belief that companies can both win at business while also being human first" (Chapter One), as opposed to "maximizing shareholder value as quickly and by any means necessary—even at the expense of employees and customers" (Chapter Three). And, while this may have embodied a way of working, it wasn't until recent years that we documented what we mean by Grow Better, and found ways to track our progress. The category creation playbook still has value long after the initial creative event.

Culture. We were a little late to the impact of culture, so I am particularly pleased to see it included as an essential part of the category creation playbook. Anthony takes a lot of the mystery out of the role of culture right from the start (Chapter Five), and ties it to real business metrics such as employee recruitment and retention. Even in companies within well-established categories, culture continues to pay dividends.

In Chapter Nine, "Activate Customers as Brand Ambassadors," Anthony employs that key word, *activate*. It should come as no surprise that as CMO of Gainsight, he finds great value in activating *successful customers*. Even so, there is a difference between successful customers and *activated* customers. With inbound marketing, we definitely ate our own dog food at HubSpot, and for sure we had some great customer advocates along the way. In more recent years, already deep into our category, we have rediscovered the value of positive customer word of mouth. We've developed actual plays to cultivate them; given them opportunities to be more vocal; and established metrics to make sure we are always moving the needle. Once again, having it as part of a playbook in the early days of category creation is a luxury I wish we had had.

There is something breathless about category creation, to "start and grow a conversation that doesn't exist yet." There is excitement enough just in that. There's no need to multiply the excitement and breathlessness with making the entire journey an exercise of trial and error. There are battle-tested practices that take some risk out of the equation. Do enough of these well, and early enough, and there is one new category more likely to appear—with your name on it.

Brian Halligan
Co-Founder and CEO at HubSpot

About the Author

Anthony Kennada is a B2C marketer trapped in a B2B body.

As the founding chief marketing officer at Gainsight, Anthony and his team are credited with creating the Customer Success category—a business imperative, profession, and software category that helps subscription companies grow sustainably by becoming customer obsessed. By focusing on human first community building, content marketing, live events, and creative activations, Anthony and his team developed a new playbook for B2B marketing that built the Gainsight brand and fueled the company's growth.

At Gainsight, Anthony was responsible for the company's global marketing strategy, including demand generation, brand and communications, product marketing, company enablement, and inside sales. He and his team created the Pulse community of Customer Success professionals, which in its first seven years welcomed over 25,000 executives to conferences on three continents and 50+ chapters of PulseLocal communities across the globe.

Gainsight has been recognized by *Forbes* as one of the top 100 private cloud companies in the world and as one of America's Most Promising Companies, by Deloitte as one of the fastest growing companies on the Technology Fast 500, by *Inc.* magazine as one of the top companies in America, and by *Fortune* magazine as one of 20 Great Workplaces in Tech.

Anthony has received the following distinctions:

- 2019 Comparably Best Marketing Leaders Award
- 2019 TOPO Summit Excellence in Marketing Award

- 2019 Data-Driven CMO Innovation Award
- 2018 DMN 40 Under 40 Award
- 2016 Pepperdine University 40 Under 40

Anthony has previously worked at Box, LiveOffice, and Symantec, and serves as an investor, advisor, and board member to enterprise software startups around the globe.

PART I

The Long–Term Greed of Category Creation

1 | Category Creation: The Noble Marketing Strategy That Can Spark a Movement

No one ignores phone calls at 9:00 p.m. on a Sunday.

That's what I thought, anyway, driving up the I-5 from Los Angeles to San Francisco. The name displayed on the phone (now on its second ring) was Nick Mehta, my former CEO who *almost never* called—certainly not this late and not this out of the blue. Before the third ring, I played the entire conversation through in my head. Having sold our last company to Symantec, perhaps Nick figured out the next chapter of his career and would offer me an opportunity to join him. Before the fourth ring, I knew I would say yes to this hypothetical job offer should it be extended, even before hello—that's just the caliber of leader in Nick Mehta.

Looking back, I sure am glad I picked up.

■ ■ ■

Maybe you can relate to my position in that story—getting the phone call for the career opportunity that could, just maybe, change your life. Perhaps as an entrepreneur or executive, you can relate to making the call and closing that dream candidate. From either point of view, something about that moment transcends our professional lives and makes an impression deep within our humanity—the prospect of being part of something great, leaving a dent in the universe, and maybe creating some personal wealth along the way.

The energy behind original ideas is electrifying. You find that you're spending hours of time (maybe even your free time) infatuated with the problem that you're looking to solve in the market, researching the competitive landscape, and filling your iPhone Notes app with ideas to bring your concept to life. But the deeper you delve into your research, you begin to make a few observations that are *different* about this concept relative to others you've had in the past:

- **There are no (or very few) competitors in the space.** That's ok though, right? You've discovered how to solve a complex problem before others have.
- **There are no analysts or media covering the space.** If you squint your eyes, one of those 2x2 quadrants *could* make sense for your concept, but doesn't really paint the full picture of the vision.
- **There exists a small and early cohort of people who believe deeply in the idea.** Well that's reassuring—but why isn't any company paying attention to them in a meaningful way?

Your excitement turns into curiosity as you turn to Google in search of best practices on how to position the company given these nuances. Clearly someone must have done this before! However, your curiosity quickly becomes a moment of panic as you realize that you are floating alone in a vast blue ocean on a pool float—that while there are some examples of companies that have done this before, there is no universally accepted playbook for *how* to launch your marketing strategy without a market to launch into. My friends, you may be in a position to create a category.

I'm here to say that this book is written for you, and that no, you're not alone on your journey. As the founding chief marketing officer at Gainsight, I found myself in the exact situation that you're in right now. My team and I have spoken to (literally) thousands of companies on our journey in building the *Customer Success* category, and the recurring theme from those conversations is that we are indeed in uncharted territory and are all figuring this out together. There's comfort in that camaraderie, but I felt that it was important to capture everything that we as an industry have learned to date on paper to help empower the next generation of marketers, founders, and executives to learn from our stories—the good, the bad, and everything in between. The result is the very book that you're holding right now, the first and only playbook on category creation written by operators for operators.

Category creation has become one of the hottest topics in marketing, and for good reason, as there's no strategy quite like it that can result in both commanding market leadership for the company on top, and incredible personal fulfillment for customers, employees, and investors who are along for the journey. In a world where private enterprise can often be mischaracterized as an at-all-cost pursuit of profit, category creation seeks to reinforce a belief that companies can both win at business while also being human first. Customers of category creators benefit from a company in the marketplace seeking to help them solve complex problems, get promoted, and self-actualize in their own lives and career journeys. Employees at category creators have a unique opportunity to unleash their creativity in the workplace, participate in an incredible corporate culture, and launch a movement behind a new product or service. Investors of category creators are typically in it for the long game, as the market will reward companies able to create and dominate new categories exponentially more than traditional disruptors.

The playbook I've compiled in this book will be primarily influenced by a business-to-business (B2B) perspective; however the tactics and strategies discussed will have broad application in the business-to-consumer (B2C) context as well. One of the main reasons for this approach is a deep belief I have that the B2B and B2C worlds are in fact merging, ushering in a new era for business that's focused on marketing, selling, and supporting the humans behind the logos that we target—otherwise known as business-to-human (B2H). I'll go into more detail on B2H in the next chapter and on how brand has moved from a deprioritized expense and distraction from growth in most businesses to becoming the heart of their business strategy.

The good news is that anyone can participate in category creation—even companies that are in their infancy or are in the early innings of bringing a product to market. While developing a 10x product is an incredible advantage (see Slack, Uber, or Airbnb as examples), it's not a prerequisite. Category creation will typically be a marketing-led exercise focused on an exciting new approach to brand positioning, content marketing, community building, and several other levers that we'll explore in detail. With that being the case, I wrote this book with two specific audiences in mind:

- **Startup Marketers or Founders in High Tech Interested in Creating a Category.** Whether or not you live in Silicon Valley, or at least subscribe to the belief that software is eating the world, you can appreciate the unique opportunity for startups to create a better future. You may be a founder or entrepreneur with a "change the world" idea that seems bigger than a single company, but the beginnings of an entirely new industry. You may be a marketer who joined a hot startup and are tasked with building a strategy to articulate your founding team's vision. This book will help shape your thinking and offer practical strategies that you can leverage to launch your company and product into a brand new market category, rather than disrupt an existing one.
- **Enterprise Marketers or Executives Operating in Commoditized Markets.** The natural course for products in established markets is toward commoditization. Consider the file sharing industry as an example: if you need to store a file online to send to a friend or colleague, there are currently 285 file storage and sharing vendors (according to G2) available to choose from. That's a great thing for consumers; however, what's good for customers is not always good for vendors

operating in crowded markets. Marketers or executives tasked with standing out in these industries may consider building, buying, or partnering their way into new product categories to expand their positioning and break away from the noise. Whether category creation is an option for this audience or not, the underlying tactics behind the strategy will give enterprise marketers the tools they need to differentiate their brands in the marketplace by focusing on the humans behind the campaigns they're driving.

Whichever camp you may be in, or even if you're someone entirely different who's interested in learning, the lessons and case studies we'll explore in this book will radically challenge conventional wisdom on how to win in business by taking the road less traveled. But before we get any further, let's define what we mean by category creation and set some context on the emerging business practice.

What Is Category Creation?

Category creation is a business strategy that focuses on positioning and evangelizing a brand new problem observed in the marketplace, in addition to the solution for that very problem. The output is an entirely new industry of products and services—distinct and differentiated from anything that had ever come before—with a single "category defining" company positioned as the winner in the new market. Category creation will typically refer to *market categories* that are aligned to a company's master brand, but for established companies, there are also cases of creating *product categories* that are aligned to a specific business unit or product line. Marketing's job in both cases, which we'll dive into at a tactical level throughout the book, will be to start and grow a conversation that doesn't yet exist—a much harder strategy that requires creativity, conviction, and a whole lot of patience.

There's been renewed excitement about category creation in recent years—likely due to the accelerating pace of commoditization in technology—although companies have been creating categories

Table 1.1 Examples of Category Creators

Category Name	Company
Inbound Marketing	HubSpot
Cloud Computing	Salesforce
Marketing Automation	Eloqua
B2B e-Commerce	Ariba
Digital Transaction Management	DocuSign
Customer Success	Gainsight
Ridesharing	Uber
Single Serve Coffee Makers	Keurig
Sports Beverages	Gatorade
Automobiles	Ford Motor Company
Photocopiers	Xerox
Video Game Consoles	Magnavox

since the beginning of industry. Table 1.1 showcases just a few examples of new categories and which companies are widely identified as their creators (although in some cases there may be debate).

One of the best examples of category creation in B2B is HubSpot, who in 2005 observed that the way consumers were interacting with marketing was fundamentally changing. Customers were increasingly doing research online to choose companies and products that would meet their needs, while outbound marketing tactics like cold calls had become interruptive and less effective. HubSpot had also been operating adjacent to two somewhat established categories—CRM with Salesforce as the incumbent, and Marketing Automation with the likes of Eloqua, Silverpop, and Infusionsoft.

The early team at HubSpot could very well have taken a challenger position against any one of the vendors within these existing categories, but made a historic decision to think about the problem in a different way. In 2009, co-founders Brian Halligan and Dharmesh Shah coined the term *Inbound Marketing* by publishing the category-defining book of the same name. The positioning was an instant hit with HubSpot's early and loyal community of customers and agency partners, but it took years (and a lot of evangelism) for the market at large to make the cognitive reference of Inbound Marketing as a proven category. One of the tactics that HubSpot deployed to win both the hearts and minds of the community was to create a catalyzing and compelling event now known as *INBOUND* to bring the industry together. This conference (which today hosts more than 24,000 attendees) has become the annual destination for the category, and a powerful platform for HubSpot to educate and empower everyone in the company and community on how to be great at Inbound Marketing. Ten years later, HubSpot is now worth over $6.6B, with 56,500 customers in over 100 countries around the world. It pays to be the category winner, but I'll get to that in a second.

Another way to define category creation is by setting context for what it is not. For years, Silicon Valley has been obsessed with the word *disruption*. The term shows up in pitch decks, conference brands, even in job titles. There's no better source for understanding disruptive technologies than Clayton Christensen's iconic bestseller, *The Innovator's Dilemma*. "Disruptive technologies bring to market a very different value proposition than had been available previously. Products based on disruptive technologies are typically cheaper, simpler, smaller, and, frequently, more convenient to use" (Christensen, 2000, p. xv). A disruption-based business strategy is antithetical to a category creation strategy, as it will typically identify an incumbent vendor in the marketplace and position a "better mousetrap" solution to the problem they solve. There are many proven best practices, books, and blogs written on how to run that play.

Disruptors will typically take a challenger position against an incumbent industry leader in order to challenge their market share. We see disruption everywhere—whether that's Zoom challenging video conference vendors such as Cisco WebEx and Citrix GoToMeeting, Box challenging establishment content management vendors such as Microsoft SharePoint and OpenText Documentum, or Salesforce's Quip challenging traditional document vendors such as Google Docs and the Microsoft Office suite.

On the other hand, category creation typically *has no incumbent vendor in the market*, and no single company articulating the problem in a way that's currently addressable by a product. The value proposition is not just different, it's brand new. So how can you tell whether to bet on a category disruption or category creation strategy? It all starts with the problem that you want to solve.

How to Tell Whether You're Creating a Category

The truth is that most entrepreneurs, executives, and marketers don't set out to create a category from the onset, but rather, see patterns in the journey of planning the business that signal there's a category to be created. These signals are observations of a unique problem in the market that no one is paying attention to in a meaningful way. It's important to note that identifying unmet need is merely the first signal of category creation (albeit an important one). Further research may suggest an entire industry already exists that's attempting to solve the problem you've identified. Table 1.2 will serve as a useful framework for understanding the six signals of category creation to determine if it's the right strategy for your business.

If the above points resonate—even a few—then category creation may be a winning strategy for your business. However, the checklist in Table 1.2 seems anything but optimistic, right? Could there really be opportunity on the other end of those signals, and if so, why not run a disruption marketing playbook instead? Doesn't that seem easier? The answer is an unquestionable yes; however, there's a bigger prize waiting for companies able to create and dominate new markets.

Why Create a Category?

Creating a category is a worthy challenge in and of itself, but in reality, the true value belongs to the company able to go on and dominate the category that they've built. However, not every category creator is the

Table 1.2 Is Category Creation the Right Strategy for You?

Signal	Yes/No
1. Little to No Competitors in Your Space—Although there may be a handful of small, early stage companies addressing a similar problem (or at the fringes), there is no incumbent "800-pound gorilla" brand that dominates the market.	
2. Low Search Volume/Cheap(er) Ad Inventory—Typically no one is searching for the problem you solve by name, which makes your ability to buy traffic exponentially harder than those operating in established markets.	
3. No Press or Media Coverage—There are no beat reporters or media outlets covering your space (although you may have some early influencers who can serve as evangelists and brand advocates).	
4. A Marginalized Buyer No Company is Paying Attention to—Do your buyers or users have power within the organization? Is there a company in the marketplace focused on making them heroes? Are they underserved?	
5. Small (but Passionate) Niche of People Who "Get It"—Are there small communities, consultants, or influencers who are out ahead of any company talking about the problem?	
6. Larger Population of People Who Don't "Get It" (Right Away)—Our brains are wired to identify cognitive references when approached with an original idea. You may find that your friends in the industry, partners, maybe even investors can't understand the full scope of your vision, but instead try to compartmentalize the vision into an existing category.	

category winner—sometimes the company that creates the category is upended by a *fast follower* who runs away with the market. In fact, there are several cautionary tales of category creators who ended up losing control of the markets they created—let's take a look at a few examples.

Do you remember the Altair 8800? This microcomputer was designed in 1974 and is widely recognized as the spark that ignited the microcomputer revolution as the first commercially successful personal computer. Its parent company MITS had virtually no competition in 1975, that is, until Steve Jobs and Steve Wozniak sold the Apple I one year later and introduced the world to the personal computer and ran away with the category as we know it today.

Do you remember the Rio PMP300? This device was one of the first portable consumer MP3 digital audio players, and certainly the first commercially successful one. The Rio was first introduced in 1998 by Diamond Multimedia and had the capability to hold approximately 10 songs at a bitrate of 128 kbit/s. Less than three years later, Apple was back as a fast follower and introduced the iPod, a revolutionary portable consumer MP3 player that could play 1000 songs (10x the capability of the Rio PMP300) at an even better bitrate.

How about search engines? Before "Google" became a verb and back when "Alexa" was just a name, the early 1990s sparked innovation in web search engine with services like Archie, Veronica, and Jughead. By the late 1990s, five players had emerged as leaders in the gold rush of commercialized online search, including Yahoo!, Magellan, Lycos, Infoseek, and Excite. The Search Engine category was one of the brightest stars of the IPO frenzy of the late 1990s, with many winners emerging in the space. That was until 2000, when a relatively unknown fast follower called Google introduced an iterative algorithm technology called PageRank that was able to accurately measure the importance of web pages. Today, Google Search is the most used search engine on the World Wide Web across all platforms, with 92.92% market share as of February 2019,[1] handling more than 3.5 billion searches each day. Sorry, Archie.

---

[1] "Search Engine Market Share Worldwide–February 2019," StatCounter, accessed March 8, 2019, http://gs.statcounter.com/search-engine-market-share

We've established that creating a category doesn't necessarily mean dominating the category—so why take on the challenge at all? The truth is that companies who are able to successfully do both realize faster growth, higher valuations, and dominant market leadership positions. According to *Harvard Business Review*, companies that were instrumental in creating their categories accounted for 53% of incremental revenue growth and 74% of incremental market capitalization growth[2] than their peer set. For startups creating categories, the value of dominating a market while scaling can lead to operational benefits as well. Nakul Mandan, Partner at Lightspeed Venture Partners said that "if you establish early leadership in a category, you have more access to funding, more resources to attract the best product, engineering, sales and marketing talent, and as a result, you will have a better chance of winning more market share over time. Accordingly, the perception of leadership definitely gets you a higher valuation multiple than your competitors."[3] From our experience at Gainsight, Nakul is absolutely right. I wish I could tell you that creating the Customer Success category was our intention all along—but that wouldn't be the real story.

Creating the Customer Success Category

No one sets out to create a category from day one—there are a series of observations that can signal that you and your company may already be on the journey.

That's what happened to me back in 2013, when I answered Nick Mehta's phone call late that Sunday night on I-5. Nick had just agreed to join a company called JBara Software as CEO, a company based in both St. Louis, Missouri, and Hyderabad, India, with about a dozen

---

[2] "Eddie Yoon and Linda Deeken, "Why It Pays to Be a Category Creator," *Harvard Business Review*, March 2013, https://hbr.org/2013/03/why-it-pays-to-be-a-category-creator

[3] Anthony Kennada, "How Investors Value New Category Creation," *Entrepreneur*, January 25, 2016, https://www.entrepreneur.com/article/254417

employees split between the two offices. Although the beginnings were humble, Nick resonated deeply with the vision for JBara painted by co-founders Jim Eberlin and Sreedhar Peddineni—that as more and more technology businesses have started selling through subscriptions, instead of regular, packaged software, companies have to focus more on keeping and growing customers over time, and not just acquiring new ones. The company had developed a SaaS product to operationalize that process across the business and had won over a handful of early adopters.

I joined about one month later as the founding "head of marketing," although title didn't really mean much when there were only a few of us at the company. My background was primarily in business development and product management, having been an early employee at Box in 2009 and leading a product team at security titan Symantec. Whether I intended to or not, I brought with me a healthy degree of first principles thinking as to how we would achieve our ambition for JBara. Eager to make an early impact, I got to work, sharing a desk with Nick at our Regus office space in San Jose.

One of our first acts as a team was to reach out to tier-one industry analysts to get some feedback on how the "experts" viewed our opportunity. We gave them demos of our product, organized briefings with our customers, and shared with them our vision for managing customers in a subscription world. When the firms shared their perspectives with us, we were surprised to see that they had completely misunderstood our vision—or at least didn't agree with the way we viewed our opportunity. Instead, they recommended we align JBara's positioning to their research disciplines—had we followed their advice, we would have taken a challenger position in categories such as:

- **Customer Support.** Typically defined as the group that does "break/fix" and often characterized as always-on-call and the people behind the 800 number. That's all well and good, but it doesn't necessarily help your customer or internal folks to whom this doesn't matter. Not to mention the dominant positions that Zendesk and Salesforce Service Cloud play in this existing category.

- **Customer Relationship Management (CRM).** CRM tools are typically recognized as solutions that impact customer acquisition—helping companies close new business rather than the renewals and expansion revenue outcomes that we help drive. Forget for a moment that Salesforce leads the pack of (literally) hundreds of vendors in the $120B market.

- **Recurring Revenue Management (RRM).** Aligned to enterprise resource planning (ERP), configure-price-quote (CPQ), and billing systems with the intention of capturing the entire workflow from creating a quote to recognizing the revenue. Sure, there's a positioning opportunity here for JBara, but our vision was more focused on the customer than on the business model itself.

None of those options felt right. We recognized, however, that one of the early users of the JBara platform was a persona with the job title of *Customer Success Managers* (CSMs)—a role created (and named) by Marc Benioff and the team at Salesforce almost 15 years ago. The role had been slowly picking up momentum in the eight years before Nick and I joined JBara, and those in the young community were filled with passion and energy when gathered together. We observed that digitally in an active LinkedIn group where CSMs would look to each other for peer-to-peer advice and best practices on business challenges. We observed that in person attending monthly meetups in various office parks around Silicon Valley.

This was a group who, at the time, was rather under-resourced and perhaps maybe even a little under-appreciated across the organization. They yearned to connect with each other, learn from each other's experiences, and develop a common language for how to do the job of Customer Success.

We recognized that there was clearly something here we couldn't ignore—an intuition that flew in the face of what the analyst community was telling us, but felt authentic to our interpretation of the problem in the market. This group of Customer Success Managers understood more than anyone else the devastating impact that churn could have on a subscription business—their careers literally depended on preventing it! We knew we had found our tribe, and by championing their success and making them feel like heroes, perhaps we could build a great company along the way.

So we rebranded the company from JBara Software to Gainsight, and decided that we would devote our marketing energy to spreading broad awareness that churn was the massive problem for subscription businesses that no one was talking about, that Customer Success was the business discipline with the charter to own it, and Gainsight was the technology platform to operationalize it. We made an early bet to focus less on positioning our solution, but to put forth more effort to advance the interests of the Customer Success profession by facilitating the exchange of best practices, building community, and ultimately creating industry around the profession that Salesforce is credited with establishing. Fast forward six and a half years later, Gainsight has become one of the fastest growing private companies in high tech, and LinkedIn has recognized Customer Success Managers as one of the most promising jobs in the United States for the second year in a row.[4]

It wasn't until about halfway into our journey at Gainsight that we recognized we had been creating a category all along. We started to see our name listed alongside companies like HubSpot, Marketo, Salesforce and Slack. We were asked to speak at conferences, sales kick-offs, meetups, and events all on the topic of category creation. We were humbled that entrepreneurs, marketers, and investors were interested in hearing our story, but also recognized that this hunger for best practices around category creation was a signal all its own. Nobody had written the playbook for how to create a category—so we figured we would document our learning, interview some of the most innovative category creators that we know, and empower the next set of entrepreneurs, marketers, and executives to take the road less traveled.

---

[4] "LinkedIn's Most Promising Jobs of 2019," LinkedIn, accessed March 8, 2019, https://blog.linkedin.com/2019/january/10/linkedins-most-promising-jobs -of-2019

I appreciate that as you read this, the concept of creating a category doesn't feel very easy—in fact, maybe it's even more intimidating now that you have more context. Despite that feeling, I want to encourage you to take the leap. Beyond any and all quantitative measures of success—financial or otherwise—there is undoubtedly a higher calling of category creation for customers in the community and employees who are enrolled in the mission. Solving a problem in the world is *so much bigger* than just selling stuff—it creates opportunity on a global scale, reduces complexity, and impacts lives whether directly or indirectly. You would be hard pressed to find a deeper sense of fulfillment for the individuals who are contributing to category leadership and culture within a company, or are the beneficiaries of that value creation within the community. Unlike any other marketing strategy, creating a category often feels like starting a movement, as you'll typically find a strong emotive component deep within its fabric.

At the heart of category creation are people—real humans who don't turn their humanity off when they show up to work every day. Understanding how to authentically build a brand that taps into the humanity of your market is a critical (and often misunderstood) part of the journey, and one that in a business-to-human (B2H) context will make all the difference between good and great companies. If you're going to learn how to create a category, the first thing you'll have to understand is why brand matters again.

2

Why Brand Is at the Heart of Category Creation in the Business-to-Human (B2H) Era

It's still dark outside as my iPhone chimes its painfully familiar tone at 6:00 a.m. I reach over to the nightstand, still half asleep, looking for the dopamine hit accompanied by the blinding light of a smartphone held inches from my face—a habit I promised myself I'd kick by now. I find the lock screen (as I do every morning) flooded with notifications, and the home screen littered with apps bearing red badges, numbered, quantifying my challenge for the next several minutes. Stronger than a doppio espresso, I begin my morning routine by clearing as many notifications as I possibly can before starting the day, working my way to the Mail app, where I know the real work awaits.

The red badge reads 124 unreads—how is that possible? It was only 34 when I went to bed the night before! I knew, however, that of the incremental 90 emails I received overnight, perhaps only three or four were actually of value and sent by a human being and not a marketing automation tool. Tapping into the app, I start my ritual of swiping left again and again, making split-second decisions on which emails are real, all before my feet hit the ground to begin my day.

I'm not proud of what I just shared, but my bet is that you've had a few mornings like this as well. This is our experience as consumers in today's digitally enabled world—our contact information ends up on a list somewhere, and companies infiltrate our inboxes with pitches in hopeful anticipation of open rates and click-throughs that will generate interest in their businesses. It's *incredibly* annoying. I get dressed, kiss my wife and daughter goodbye, and walk out the front door to drive into work, and instantly, *I become that annoying marketer* behind the email campaigns.

For the past several decades, B2B marketers like me have ignored the fact that behind every logo that we intend to market and sell to is a real human being—people with real wants and needs that aren't left at the door when they get to work each morning. Perhaps "ignore" is a strong word, but the reality is that we use language like "bounty boards," "hunting elephants," and "closing logos" rather than considering the people behind the companies that we market and sell to. Meanwhile, in our consumer lives, we reject the very same tactics that we deploy at work and are drawn instead to emotive companies that speak to our humanity and serve us in our journey through life. Perhaps it's taking that Virgin Atlantic flight rather than the United long haul. Maybe it's the confidence in paying full price for the Tesla Model 3 rather than haggling with that Audi salesperson on the A5. Our friends in the B2C world define this concept as brand—and *in B2C, brand is everything.*

Brand is more than just visual design, creative and advertising campaigns. Seth Godin, author and recognized brand expert, defines it as "a set of expectations, memories, stories, and relationships that, taken together, account for a consumer's decision to choose one product or service over another." By that definition, the imperative to prioritize brand in B2B marketing cannot be debated—but in practice it has been marginalized, disconnected from growth, and deprioritized in favor of automation and scale. In short, we've taken the humanity out of marketing, and customers have started to take notice.

The Imperative of Brand in Category Creation

A common attribute of category creation—regardless of vertical, industry, or region—is a human being with an unmet need. In Chapter One, we referenced a "marginalized buyer no company is paying attention to in a meaningful way" as a potential signal of category creation. One of the primary objectives on your journey will be to develop a brand that authentically recognizes and serves your audience as heroes, stokes conviction behind the problem you aim to solve together, and equips them with the tools, resources, and opportunities to self-actualize within the new industry you are creating.

A disruption-oriented marketer would take a product marketing approach to building that brand—creating content around product feature benefit, building competitive landing pages, and hosting a user conference to give customers an exclusive look at the upcoming roadmap. A category-oriented marketer, on the other hand, would create content on how to solve complex problems that the audience is challenged with, ignore the competition, and plan an industry event to bring the community together to learn and grow. The marketer in the former example is focused inward on the company and product, while the latter is focused outward on the market and customer. Table 2.1 gives a few more examples of the difference between disruption and category brand programs.

Table 2.1   Disruption-Oriented vs. Category-Oriented Brand Programs

Disruption	Category
Customer conference	Industry conference
Blogs on product use cases	Blogs on industry best practices
Field events with demos	Field events for community
Paid ads on competitor keywords	Organic ranking on category keywords
Customer advocates	Brand fanatics

As the market starts to interact with the various programs and campaigns you're running in the second column, they're getting value from your brand and enrolling into your thought leadership—all (typically) without buying anything. They become a captive audience listening to what you have to say, establishing trust in your point of view as an expert in the category, even if they're not ready to buy anything quite yet. Your products and solutions are critically important in serving customers when they're in-market for solutions, but make no mistake, your brand is where the real enterprise value resides in category creation.

One of the best examples of brand as a function of creating a category is Salesforce. In the company's early days, they articulated and evangelized an "end of software" mission that sparked a global movement behind the Cloud Computing category that, according to Gartner, is a market projected to grow 17.3 percent in 2019 to total $206.2 billion, up from $175.8 billion in 2018.[1] While they positioned the brand around "ending" software, the company was actually in market with a CRM product for sales teams, punching above their weight and aligning their brand with a movement. Salesforce CEO Marc Benioff details his approach to building the Salesforce brand in his now iconic memoir *Behind the Cloud*, including how creating a "NO SOFTWARE" logo helped articulate their differentiation in the marketplace. The company's product portfolio (which has evolved over the years) is impressive, but their brand is the reason they're the world's most valuable public cloud company with over $120B of market cap and have been recognized on *Fortune*'s World's Most Admired Companies List for six years in a row.

In *Behind the Cloud*, Benioff underscores the importance of brand on category creation with a master class for entrepreneurs and marketers inspired by the Salesforce playbook. Professionals were tired of using software to be productive at work—especially in increasingly

---

[1] "Gartner Forecasts Worldwide Public Cloud Revenue to Grow 17.3 Percent in 2019." Gartner, September 2018, https://www.gartner.com/en/newsroom /press-releases/2018-09-12-gartner-forecasts-worldwide-public-cloud-revenue -to-grow-17-percent-in-2019

mobile disciplines such as Sales, where they were constantly away from their desks. Benioff writes that Salesforce owns "NO SOFTWARE— not because [they] are the only one doing it but because [they] were the first to think it was important to customers" (Benioff, 2009, p. 32). While this fact can surely be disputed, Salesforce's end of software mission effectively created the Cloud Computing category, which along with advances in mobile devices, hosted infrastructure, and communications technology has enabled an entire economy of working professionals to be productive from anywhere in the world, and from any device.

How Did We Get Here?

The concept of brand marketing can be traced back to the 1950s with consumer packaged goods companies like Procter & Gamble, General Foods, and Unilever. Madison Avenue and the American advertising industry were peaking in popularity, although advertising in America had already been around for nearly 100 years by that point. Brand managers were developing the art of giving products an identity that distinguished them from the competition—articulating both functional and emotional value. A binge session of AMC's *Mad Men* on Netflix should provide all the historical context you need on the early years of brand (and maybe a bit more societal context to boot).

However in the late 20th century, the now globalized economy experienced a massive disaggregation of business that created industry around specialist providers in the value chain who could help enable end products for consumers. The two main focal points of specialization included product development (become an expert in manufacturing something) and logistics (become an expert in getting products from one place to another). Take, for instance, personal computers, which leveraged specialized components from product manufacturers around the globe, as well as logistics support, to get the computers in the hands of the customer. Supply was the scarcity of the time, which ushered in the era of B2B commercial transactions and, officially, B2B marketing as a discipline.

The early chapters of B2B marketing were quite traditional, with the company at the center of the marketing model with messages flowing outward through different channels, including TV, direct mail, fax, newspaper, outdoor, and radio. There were limited opportunities for input back to the company and cross-channel messaging. In this world, brand was indeed important, but completely disconnected from how B2B companies drove deals through the supply chain. This was, of course, until the Internet became mainstream in the mid-1990s and everything as we know it changed.

In the Internet era, it was no longer supply that was scarce, but rather customers. Companies recognized the land grab for customers in this new Internet gold rush as B2B marketers began to build websites, leverage early search tools, and create integrated marketing campaigns to re-aggregate consumer experiences across all channels. The economic premium shifted away from product and distribution, and toward creating world-class experiences for the end consumers. As businesses began to standardize on email as the primary means of communication, a new category was born in Marketing Automation to help companies amplify the impact of analog marketing by an exponential factor, provide air cover for sales, and create personalized campaigns that engaged the long tail of customers.

Marketing Automation is arguably one of the most successful new categories in B2B for both vendors and consumers. On the vendor side, Eloqua (the category creator) had an incredible outcome by going public in 2012 before getting acquired by Oracle later that year for $810M. Marketo, one of the fast followers behind Eloqua, went public in 2013 at a $724M market cap before getting acquired by Adobe in 2018 for a whopping $4.75B. There were several other winners in the category, including HubSpot (IPO), Silverpop (acquired by IBM), and Pardot and ExactTarget (both acquired by Salesforce). Customers won and the category became inevitable, as chief marketing officers evolved from corporate marketers to demand generators, earning a seat at the executive table and the majority share of operating budget in B2B businesses. Marketing became widely recognized as a critical part of the growth equation. However, as marketers built demand gen organizations and implemented marketing automation systems in their businesses, the email channel became incredibly noisy, fracturing once again the end consumer experience that the promise of B2B marketing hoped to optimize. That's the world we find ourselves in as a profession today—eager to find better ways to rise above the noise, deliver meaningful value, and stand out in the marketplace.

Enter Business-to-Human (B2H) Marketing

In the mid-to-late 2000s, the workforce became mobile as the launch of the iPhone put the power of a supercomputer into our pockets. Consider this—the whole idea of "leaving work at the office" was never really a choice until smartphones broke down most barriers to connectivity. Today, work-life balance and integration are foundational mental health disciplines that, according to the American Psychological Association, can affect organizational outcomes such as productivity, absenteeism, and turnover.

However, we do benefit from this connectivity and digital awareness in our consumer lives on an almost daily basis—the ability to watch movies or listen to music with the touch of a button using Netflix and Spotify, connect with friends and family across the globe with social networks such as Facebook and LinkedIn, and purchase almost any product in the world and have it arrive on our doorstep in 48 hours or less with Amazon Prime. This is the expectation in the marketplace that speaks to the very essence of our humanity—to be entertained, to foster community, to save time and money. Yet when we step back into the office, we forget these things and the humanity of our audience and are instead back into the familiar rhythm of email cadences, cold calls, and marketing funnels.

What would it look like instead if B2B marketers could realize that the people listening to music on Spotify and buying products on Amazon at home, are the same executive sponsors or power users of the opportunity record in your CRM currently forecasted to close at $200K? What if the same tactics and channels that B2C brands leverage to drive acquisition and engagement can be used to build affinity with a B2B audience? Perhaps the craziest statement of all, what if this new way to market actually helped close that deal, drive growth for the company, and align your brand with the category you're creating?

What I'm framing above is an argument for a new way of thinking about marketing and selling business services called business-to-human (B2H)—a human-first strategy that seeks to drive business growth by serving the individuals behind the logos. The underlying belief of B2H is that customers will choose to work with companies they trust and admire, especially if they are the market leaders. There are several trends that have established B2H marketing as less of a platitude, and more of a viable business strategy:

- **Proliferation (and Commoditization) of Digital Products.** With most new products coming to market as "born in the cloud" services, it's becoming easier to launch new technology into the marketplace. Therefore, customers now have more choice than ever before and can likely find an alternative viable solution to migrate to if a specific vendor cannot meet their needs. As an example from Chapter One, if you need to share a large file online, there are an overabundance of vendors in the file sync and share market who can help you with that.
- **Subscription (or Pay-Per-Use) Business Model.** Freemium and free trial motions have made it an order of magnitude easier for vendors to acquire new customers, now that the threshold for trying new services has been lowered. Solutions like Uber and Lyft, or even Amazon Web Services, only realize revenue on a pay-per-use or consumption basis, moving all of the power in the economic equation away from vendors and toward the customer.
- **Voice of the Customer on Social Media.** It may sound obvious, but customers now have more voice than ever before.

If they feel any sense of dissatisfaction with a brand, they will happily take to social media to voice their displeasure. Online review platforms such as Capterra, G2, and TrustRadius are creating platforms to centralize customer voice for software purchase decisions.

- **The Digitally Empowered Buyer.** A trend first observed by HubSpot, prospects are spending much more time researching your brand online before ever engaging in a sales process. According to Forrester, 60% of today's business buyers prefer not to interact with a sales rep as the primary source of information, 68% prefer to research on their own online, and 62% say they can now develop selection criteria or finalize a vendor list based solely on digital content.[2]
- **Content Creation and Distribution Capability.** The technology needed to create high fidelity content has become more accessible and cost effective, arguably with iPhone leading the way. This has resulted in new channels and programs that are relevant to both B2B and B2C brands, including podcasting, live streaming, social "stories" and several others.

A B2H marketing strategy is equal parts philosophy and practice—philosophy as it pertains to the narrative that you develop to engage with your audience, and practice as it pertains to the channels that you leverage to reach them. The underlying principle of the philosophy is defining the narrative in service of the individuals rather than the companies they work for: how can I help them solve problems, meet peers and mentors, and earn a seat at the executive table? These themes will undoubtedly come up as you develop a content marketing strategy. The practice can reflect many of the same content form factors that have become commonplace in the market to date—blogs, e-books, live events, webinars, direct mail, etc.—but can also be re-imagined to reach your audience in other channels where they

---

[2] Lori Wizdo, "The Ways and Means of B2B Buyer Journey Maps: We're Going Deep at Forrester's B2B Forum." Forrester, August 2017, https://go.forrester.com /blogs/the-ways-and-means-of-b2b-buyer-journey-maps-were-going-deep-at -forresters-b2b-forum/

spend time. At Gainsight, we came up with an admittedly crazy idea to record a hip-hop single about Customer Success and distribute through Spotify, Apple Music, and other major music publishers. I'll explain the rationale behind the idea in Chapter Seven, but at the end of the day, our intention is to build a brand that *does life* with the people in our category, even if that means giving them a song to listen to on their way into work.

This whole approach intuitively made a lot of sense to me (maybe as a millennial in the workforce or something), but early in my time at Gainsight, I felt like my peers in the industry looked at me as though I was crazy. The conventional wisdom of the time around B2B marketing was to run the proven playbook—SEO/SEM, lead scoring, email nurture, and outbound calls. There were plenty of blog posts and resources on disciplines like sales development, growth hacking, and account-based marketing. These tactics were supposedly the secret to fast growth in B2B, not brand. Yet as our campaigns began to work, and our funnel began to grow, I concluded that rumors of the demise of brand had been greatly exaggerated, that the belief that brand was disconnected from growth was widespread, viewed as a complete distraction for startups. Here's the usual argument:

- "We're focused on growth now—we'll figure out brand later."
- "I can't prove the ROI of brand."
- "I've got an agency/intern/junior content writer on that."

I'm not sure where this perspective came from, but it was everywhere. I found the exact opposite to be true about brand and its effect on our growth at Gainsight. The truth is, if you asked anybody affiliated with Gainsight where much of our success had come from, they would rattle off a number of items that would all categorically fall under brand: our thought leadership helped align Gainsight with the movement we were creating in Customer Success, our content drove organic traffic to our web properties and led the growth of our marketable database, and our community became a platform for the industry to connect together and advance the discipline forward. These investments have been instrumental to our ability to create the Customer Success category, and paradoxically has led to more than just revenue or logo growth, but even to follow-on rounds of funding, customer satisfaction, employee recruitment, and teammate retention.

In the end we may not all succeed in building the next Salesforce, but we can and should leverage the B2H strategies that they and other iconic brands have deployed in their category creation journey. By focusing on helping the humans behind the logos we sell to solve complex problems in an authentic way, we are no longer contributing to the noise that awaits us in our iPhone Mail app every morning. Rather, we are fulfilling the original intent of B2B marketing in the first place—to create integrated, world class experiences for our audience that champions their success in our category. If we focus on just that alone, two outcomes are almost certain to occur—we will be laying the foundation for a pioneering new category with our brand in the leadership position, and we will fuel our growth engine with prospects who will give us a shot at their business when they're ready to start an evaluation.

At the end of the day, success in new markets will come down to execution for all companies, regardless of whether you're an established brand or a startup. Your ability to build a brand that customers, employees, and investors will love is at the heart of creating new industries and realizing the economic outcomes of market leadership within them. The upside of creating a category is clear—exponential value, both quantitative and qualitative, when compared to companies bringing only incremental innovations to market. So why isn't every company in the modern economy attempting category creation? Well, it turns out it's not easy. In fact, it's brutally hard when compared to the disruption playbook that we've been embracing as an industry for the last several decades. The intention of the rest of the book is to introduce a new playbook, influenced by some of the best category creators of our time, to support your business as you bravely go down this path. But before we get into the tactics, it's important that you understand what you're getting yourself into.

3

The Six Challenges of Creating a Category (and How to Overcome Them)

Gustave "Gus" Levy was a college dropout from New Orleans who moved to New York City in 1928 to pursue a career in finance. Levy joined Goldman Sachs in 1933 as a trader on the foreign bond desk for a salary of $27.50 a week. Thirty-six years later, he became senior partner, ushering in a golden age at Goldman of international expansion and an increased tolerance to take on trading risk.

History will remember Levy as one of the most respected executives on Wall Street, but beyond his contributions to Goldman Sachs and the financial industry as a whole, he coined what would become an iconic adage that still echoes through the hallways of the investment banking juggernaut to this day. "Greedy," Levy would say, "but long-term greedy."

While the word "greedy" is rather notorious in nature, identified as one of the seven deadly sins and declared "good" by fictional villain Gordon Gekko in the 1987 film *Wall Street*, the spirit of Levy's iconic phrase has powerful application in modern business.

Companies that are short-term greedy are almost always outlasted by the long-term greedy. Short-term greed conjures up examples of businesses looking to maximize shareholder value quickly and by any means necessary—even at the expense of employees and customers. Several case studies come to mind, including many Internet businesses in the period between March 11, 2000, to October 9, 2002, now known as the dot-com crash. Perhaps a slightly more principled business that's short-term greedy today would focus on acquisition as a target exit strategy in order to create quick wealth and notoriety for the founding team.

Companies that are long-term greedy, on the other hand, are not interested in taking any shortcuts on their path to success. They are driven by creating lasting value in the marketplace, doing the right thing by teammates and customers, and realizing the full potential of their vision, regardless of the amount of time that it takes to do so. This is especially novel thinking in technology, where the late-1990s and mid-2010s have been characterized by a surge in M&A activity, larger-than-life corporate valuations, and a frothy venture capital environment—creating widespread religion across Silicon Valley around short-term greed.

Despite the pervasiveness of that mindset, the truth is that long-term greed has become a prerequisite of success in modern businesses. An analysis of high-growth software IPOs in 2018 by Alex Clayton, Growth Enterprise Investor at Spark Capital, found that it took companies an average of 14 years[1] from founding to the public markets (see Figure 3.1). Looking past time frame, public software-as-a-service (SaaS) companies today are "~$200M+ in ARR and growing ~40%, have ~75% GAAP gross margins, are losing money, have a 120% net dollar expansion rate, sell a ~$30K product, have almost 1,000 employees, have raised $300M from investors (and burned through at least $200M of it), and sold over $250M of stock in an IPO at a valuation of ~$2B." This data certainly paints a

---

[1] Alex Clayton, "2018 Review: High-growth SaaS IPOs," Medium, December 2018, https://medium.com/@alexfclayton/2018-review-high-growth-saas-ipos-5b82a93295c

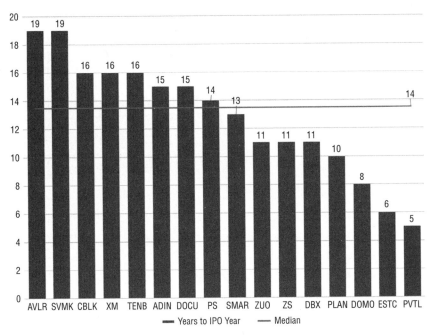

Figure 3.1   Years to IPO; Founding Year to IPO Year

different and humbling picture than the get-rich-quick perception of startup fame in Silicon Valley.

However, the truth is that an IPO is merely a financing event. Jason Lemkin, founder of SaaStr—a social community of 500,000+ SaaS founders and executives—has pushed his audience to go even longer than the 14-year IPO journey in pursuit of what he calls building a *generational company.* Lemkin believes that achieving "unicorn" status and going public is only one milestone on a company's long journey to becoming generational at $1B+ of ARR. Iconic brands such as Salesforce, ServiceNow, and Workday are already there, while others such as Box, DocuSign, and Zendesk are well on their way.

Embarking on a journey of category creation requires ***even more*** long-term greed than the average SaaS IPO. Sure, that greed could manifest itself in time-to-liquidity (don't count on a quick exit), but in reality, there are several factors that make category creation extremely difficult relative to disrupting existing markets. Let's explore six challenges of creating a category as well as some key considerations to overcome them. While this list may sound daunting (because it is), going into your journey with eyes wide open will serve you well.

1. Not Everyone Will Get It Right Away

Recall from the first chapter that one of the primary aims of category creation is to position and evangelize a new problem that you've observed in the marketplace—often a problem that customers don't even recognize they have yet. It's hard enough to position your own company and product, let alone create a cognitive reference for an entire industry. This is the intellectual challenge marketing will wrestle with throughout the journey—balancing category marketing effort of defining (and naming) the problem, with product and demand marketing effort to position the company and product as the solution. At times, it may feel like your category is *another product* in and of itself.

Over the years at Gainsight, we've spent a lot of time (and money) to help the world understand what Customer Success actually is. Many of our programs required two parallel work streams—positioning Customer Success (the category) and then also positioning Gainsight (the company and product). An example would be a quantitative ROI study we conducted early in our journey that required extra scope than perhaps a traditional business. We partnered with a third-party research firm to help us quantify the pain of churn in subscription companies, as well as unrealized expansion revenue and scaling challenges that would justify an investment in the practice of Customer Success.

Among other takeaways, the study proved that companies who adopted Customer Success programs reported a significant boost in sales revenues to the tune of an additional $11M over a three-year period. Now that we had a compelling argument we could evangelize in the marketplace, we wanted to prove the *incremental* value of using Gainsight to operationalize the Customer Success effort. The

Figure 3.2   Gainsight Highway Billboard Circa 2013

study proved that Customer Success teams who used Gainsight were able to reduce churn on average by 5–10x relative to their peer set, while also finding an average of $1M—$5M per year of operational savings by using our technology to scale. You better believe I took out a billboard on the most influential stretch of highway in the world to evangelize that value (seriously, check out Figure 3.2).

Even if you think billboards are stupid (although I'll try to convince you otherwise in a later chapter), the meta point is that getting people to believe that what you've observed is indeed a problem in the market—by name—is *extremely* difficult. A signal of your success in time will be recognizing that you're not the only one screaming your category name into a void, but rather others in the marketplace are starting to refer to it accurately as well. The challenge is that even when you start seeing your category name out there in the wild, the hard work is only getting started.

2. Customers Are Initially Interested in Education, Not Your Product

One of the realities you'll have to embrace in category creation is the imperative to educate the market through your various marketing channels. No other marketing strategy will place as big an emphasis on education as this one. Once you've developed a good content marketing program (which we'll cover in great detail in Chapters Six and Seven) and are able to capture the market's attention on the "why" behind your category, those who are listening will look to you for answers on the "how," which include a logical next set of questions, such as:

- Is *CATEGORY X* relevant to me?
- How can I convince my CEO that *CATEGORY X* is important?
- Do I need to build a team to take on a *CATEGORY X* program?
- What's a sample job description that I can use to recruit talent?
- How do I prove the value of *CATEGORY X* on revenue?
- Etc.

This is where the bulk of your content marketing effort will be spent—defining the best practices in the category you're creating, so that anyone seeking information on the category can quickly and easily find resources online, and more importantly, that the value delivery is attributed to your brand. Nothing is more important in the age of the digitally empowered buyer. Do this right, and a few things will happen: (1) your brand becomes aligned with the category you're creating in a thought leadership position, and (2) you begin to build an opt-in database of conversions from an audience listening to what you have to say. This strategy should feel somewhat familiar—this is the Inbound Marketing playbook that HubSpot has evangelized. The bet is that if your brand can act as a partner in strategy definition in the market at scale, when companies are ready to evaluate solutions, they'll engage your team in a sales process, having already received value from your content and perceived you as a trusted partner all along.

The reality is that this is extremely hard to do—especially in the early days when finding time or resources to create high-quality content is difficult. You'll feel like you're spending more time creating content about the category than your own products, a feeling you need to become very comfortable with. For a time at Gainsight, we even moved product marketing into the Product organization to focus Marketing's efforts on category marketing programs. While that tradeoff had its own set of challenges, it was the right thing to do for where we were at the time as a business.

What happens next is arguably the most difficult challenge in category creation—a phenomenon that I'm calling the ***two funnel effect***. A well-executed marketing strategy will create broad awareness of your new category and enroll the masses into your brand and thought leadership by building your marketable database (funnel one). As the market leader in the new category, you'll run a number of programs against your database that we'll cover in Part II, driving engagement from your audience as they mature in the new category. Whether through lead scoring, account-based marketing principles, or by some other measure, you'll identify signals of buying intent from your audience and attempt to engage them in a product-oriented discussion (funnel two). However, for category creators, the chasm between funnel one (interest in the category) and funnel two (interest in the product) can become quite wide. It's common to find that you've won the hearts of your audience by selling them on the problem, but are yet to win their minds by selling them on your product as the solution. We'll go into greater detail on how to bridge this chasm in Chapter Twelve, but there are several factors that contribute to the distance between the two funnels:

- Buyer is still in strategy definition mode and not yet ready for product
- Buyer needs to hire a key executive or team prior to selecting an enabling product
- Buyer is not empowered to make the purchasing decision
- Buyer doesn't know how to buy product to solve this problem (never had an opportunity to)

While the *two funnel effect* will certainly require focus to overcome—as well as tight Sales and Marketing alignment—there is good news here. Building a great funnel one will create a competitive moat around your brand unlike any other tactic, as customers generally prefer to do business with the market leader. Marketing is primarily responsible for building funnel one, as well as closing the divide into funnel two—which takes me to the next challenge.

3. You'll Need a LOT of Capital (Although There Are Workarounds)

Ariba was founded in 1996 on the idea that the Internet could be leveraged to enable companies to facilitate and improve the procurement process. Their software helped companies buy the things they needed to operate—everything from pens to vehicle fleets. You would be remiss, even back in 1996, to find a less sexy market or buyer than procurement. That was the founding team's signal, who invested significantly to create the B2B e-Commerce category, fueling Ariba to a $4B IPO in 1999 before being acquired by SAP in 2012 for $4.3B. Fun fact, Ariba was the first B2B Internet IPO in history.

But making procurement sexy did not come cheap. In the years prior to their IPO, Ariba spent $46.4M in sales and marketing efforts before generating more than $200M in revenue.[2] As referenced in Figure 3.3, the company over-invested early as a percentage of revenue to create the level of awareness required to spark the flywheel for their category. The company's annual sales and marketing budget increased by 6x YoY after their IPO to $230M and $298M in 2000 and 2001. Although the bubble burst in 2001, dropping Ariba's stock price dramatically to its IPO level, the company endured as the largest independent procurement software business and was acquired by SAP at the highest historical multiple of any software company at that point in history.

Although Ariba's story is quite historic, the lesson applies to all companies who are creating a category. The amount of capital required to create a broad level of awareness around a need that people don't know they have is non-trivial. It's no surprise that in new categories the eventual winner is the best-funded, as resources in the early days help category creators (and frankly fast followers

---

[2] Tomasz Tunguz, "From $800k to $274M in 4 Years—The Story of Ariba," May 2015, https://tomtunguz.com/ariba-history/

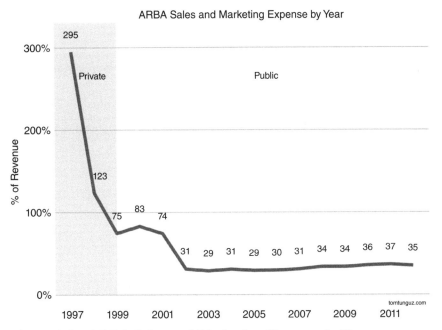

Figure 3.3   ARBA Sales and Marketing Expense by Year

as well) distance themselves from the competition. Alex Clayton's research on high-growth SaaS IPOs in 2018 found a median of $300M of equity capital raised in the private markets before going public.[3] Eventually all businesses—whether category creators or disruptors—will have to become more capital efficient and manage sales and marketing expense against industry benchmarks. But especially in the early days, companies need to fight risk aversion and invest in marketing programs that will build the foundation for new industry. However there's a complicating factor for category creators that will challenge thinking on how to deploy capital, even in cavalier ways.

---

[3] Alex Clayton, "2018 Review: High-Growth SaaS IPOs," Medium, December 2018, https://medium.com/@alexfclayton/2018-review-high-growth-saas-ipos -5b82a93295c

A Note for Bootstrapped Startups

It's important for me to recognize at this point that there are many early stage companies that may resonate with what I've written so far on category creation, but have felt a sense of defeat after reading the last section on capital. Silicon Valley, where I work, is in almost every case the exception and not the norm. Access to angel and early stage venture capital, top-tier talent, and innovation-centric educational institutions are only some of the characteristics that give Silicon Valley an unfair advantage on the rest of the world. You can probably go down the list and argue a similar position for New York City, Seattle, Austin, and other emerging secondary markets in the United States.

The reality is that not every company has equal access to capital; however we all possess equal ambition to create big visions for our businesses. If you are bootstrapping your company, or are in the early days of putting your concept together, I want you to know that this book is also written for you. As we dive into the "Seven Principles to Create (and Dominate) a Category" in Part II, we will walk through a detailed playbook on how to execute a category creation strategy. Some of the ideas will seem capital intensive (e.g., create an industry conference of record for your category), but most will feel achievable with the right balance of priority and scale. I will make sure to provide examples and case studies of capital efficient ways of executing the same playbook as we delve into each topic. Following these principles can put your company in a position to generate enough sustainable growth to either self-fund your future or take in outside funding to scale later down the road.

The truth is wherever you are geographically, and with little or no institutional funding, you can still create a category and build a generational company along the way. Don't believe me? In 2002, a college student named Ryan Smith decided to build an online research company with his father from his parents' basement in Provo, Utah. They targeted the academia market, arguably one of the toughest verticals, with little budget and extremely long sales cycles. Ten years later in 2012, they took their first round of funding after Accel and Sequoia had been knocking down their door for three years. Days before their IPO in November 2018, Ryan Smith, his father, and the rest of the Qualtrics team were acquired by SAP for $8B in cash. When asked about that decision to take institutional investment back in 2012, Ryan had this to say: "One plus one has to equal five. If one plus one doesn't equal five, this deal doesn't work. It has to be so compelling to achieve our objectives that we're all in. We got Sequoia and Accel and that's exactly what happened."[4]

Ryan Smith and Qualtrics are creating the Experience Management (XM) category, and for the most part, have been extremely successful while bootstrapping the business from over 800 miles away from Palo Alto. It may have taken them 16 years—which relative to the 14-year median of 2018's IPO class is somewhat within range—but they've built a generational business that flies in the face of Silicon Valley consensus.

4. Short-Term Planning Is Extremely Hard

Marketing attribution and sales forecasting are hard enough when your business can identify and pursue a market using BANT (Budget, Authority, Needs, and Timeline) as a qualification framework. However, when you're creating a category, you can pretty much count on throwing BANT out the window—or at least BAT. Here's why:

- **Budget.** For new categories, it's common that your buyer has never procured software (or other purpose-built products) to

---

[4] Derek Andersen, "The Story Behind Qualtrics, the Next Great Enterprise Company." TechCrunch, March 2013, https://techcrunch.com/2013/03/02/the-story-behind-qualtrics-the-next-great-enterprise-company/

solve this problem before and will need to find the dollars from elsewhere in the budget.

- **Authority.** In many cases, your buyer is either not empowered to make purchasing decisions, or otherwise needs to build a business case up the org chart in order to do a deal.
- **Timeline.** Buying a product is only one part of category creation as prospects are still wrapping their heads around the problem, defining their strategy, and building their team to take the charter.

Qualifying need is critical, but exponentially more difficult in new categories due to the *two funnel effect* I introduced earlier. The cost to acquire a conversion in funnel one is high enough, never mind how to bridge that conversion into funnel two, and eventually as a paid customer of your product. So without a proven attribution or sales qualification framework to benchmark against, how do you justify investments in category marketing?

5. Executives and Investors Need to Buy In or You Will Fail

Without any question, category creation starts at the top—you need both an executive team and set of investors who are patient, have bought into the mission, and are long-term greedy. The challenges we're establishing in this chapter are non-trivial, and require decision making and strategic planning at the CEO and board level—without it, the category marketing programs I'll advocate running throughout the book will not be funded, or almost certainly abandoned if without quick results. The threat of confirmation bias in management is especially applicable as the teams you'll build and investors you engage would likely have spent more time operating and funding market disruptors rather than market creators. Sales quarters can be bumpy, CAC ratios out of whack in the early innings, but building something amazing requires patience, courage, and conviction. This also shows up in the culture you build within your sales organization—prototypical AEs who are used to "set 'em up and knock 'em down" sales processes will either need to be converted or weeded out of the organization—otherwise they will happily leave on their own. I can't understate how important culture is to building a new category, a topic we'll go into in Chapters Five and Thirteen.

If you need to convince your leadership or investors to take the leap and create a category, you may be playing from behind already. The impact to enterprise valuation and business growth that I summarized in Chapter One alone should set the stage on your behalf, but identifying the signals within your own company and building your business case accordingly should push them over the edge. Remember that category and brand marketing fundamentally drive growth—arguably in a much more sustainable way than traditional methods. Ultimately, the ability to attribute every marketing activity to a funnel metric is critical to proving the ROI of category marketing efforts and getting budget approval to run more plays.

We'll go into the specifics in Chapter Twelve, but down-funnel metrics such as sales forecasting get more predictive in time as your category matures—developing a common language and point of view as a revenue team is important to keep executives aligned on the mission, and the CFO supportive of adding fuel in the form of budget dollars to the fire that you're sparking.

6. Understanding the Competition Is Confusing

While one of the signals of category creation is no identified incumbent in the market, there are often small companies that either compete directly or compete at the fringes that will eventually adopt your category positioning once traction is made. However, in new markets, it's really not about the competition, but rather all about the market itself. The true competition for category creators, especially in the early days, is creating enough inertia to will the market into existence—and being ignorant enough to not be distracted by what the competition is doing.

While it may seem counterintuitive, competition is actually a critical component to the success of new markets—otherwise inviting the criticism of whether or not it's a real category at all. How you choose to engage your competition, however, is a calculated decision that each company should make itself. Within Gainsight's core business, we made the decision to respectfully "ignore" the competitors in our young category and focus primarily on building the market while positioning our brand as the thought leader. We chose to take up as much of the oxygen in Customer Success as we could, recognizing that there were other vendors in our market who were contributing to the conversation as well.

Other companies stand by a different approach—take Mark Organ, CEO and founder of Influitive and creator of the Advocate Marketing category (Mark was also the founder of Eloqua, the creators of the Marketing Automation category). Mark believes that for category creators, co-opetition trumps competition, as the primary responsibility of the leader is to enlarge the collective total addressable market (TAM). At Influitive, Mark and team spent over $1M to put their competitors on stage as speakers and sponsors of their industry event for Advocate Marketing called Advocamp. Mark believes that losing deals to the competition is a better alternative than losing to status quo, as it means demand for the category is growing.

In either approach, the way you choose to rationalize the competitive landscape in new categories will be fundamentally different from taking a challenger position against an incumbent player in an existing market. You may not necessarily see each other in every deal, but you are in a sense competing for thought leadership. Customers and prospects are building affinity with the different vendors in the marketplace through content and evangelism efforts, whether they're paying customers yet or not.

At this point, if you are a startup founder or marketer interested in creating a category from the ground up, I want to give you permission to skip ahead to Chapter Five, where we'll dive into the playbook with 10 principles to create (and dominate) a category—proven strategies as shared by some of the leading category creators in the modern economy.

I want to talk directly to the enterprise marketers and executives, who may be excited at the prospect of creating a category, but are grounded in the reality of working at a company currently operating in a crowded market. The truth is that you have an opportunity to either (a) reposition your established brand around a new market category by building, partnering, or buying your way into a new (or emerging) product category or (b) leverage a certain set of *unfair advantages* that you possess over startup competitors to re-imagine your brand in a B2H context. Those are the options we'll explore, and the playbook we'll dive into in Part II will be just as valid to you and your teams. But before we get to that, there are a few nuances for established brands that are worth disclosing.

4 | Special Considerations for Established Companies in Commoditized Markets

The year is 2012 and the team at Amazon is busy asserting their dominance as the web's largest retailer by invading any tangential territory even slightly related to their business. The company had just released new e-book readers and tablet hardware, acquired a book publishing company, and even opened up a social gaming studio. While these investments may seem a few steps removed from their core retail business, Amazon CEO Jeff Bezos is intentionally and masterfully executing his plan of building a content ecosystem of apps, books, music, and movies as a competitive moat around the Amazon brand.

Within the core business, the historic success of Amazon had ushered in for the market at large what some commentators have referred to as the "retail apocalypse." The Amazon effect was felt across both Main Street and Wall Street, as mom-and-pop stores were forced to embrace the rising e-commerce trend, while major big-box stores were at the risk of going out of business by losing to the convenience that Amazon introduced to the market. From 2015 to 2019, over 68 major retailers filed for bankruptcy, according to CB Insights,[1] citing issues such as mounting losses and drops in sales. One of the companies caught in Amazon's cross-hairs was Best Buy, who seemed to be one of the last electronics retailers standing after the collapse of Circuit City, CompUSA, RadioShack, and others. Best Buy was bleeding money as customers would come into the store to test products they were interested in only to buy them later online on Amazon at a cheaper price.

Seven years later, not only is Best Buy still alive, but the company is *thriving*—reporting strong results in fiscal 2019, beating guidance last quarter by generating $14.8B of revenue, and offering a solid outlook for fiscal 2020. It wasn't just Best Buy, but other retailers such as Costco and Kohls redefined their businesses in the shadows of the retail apocalypse and as a result are winning in the market. How did they do it? Also, what do their stories tell us about the market conditions that put them on their heels in the first place?

The Commoditization of Industry

The retail apocalypse has proven that it's not just products, but entire industries that can become commoditized. Consider the Cloud Computing category that we referenced in Chapter Two—born out of a noble "end of software" movement that today has become the primary method for developing and distributing business and consumer applications. There are distinct similarities between the commoditization of the retail and software industries, as well as other categories such as transportation and energy storage—the arrival of breakthrough innovation and new business models that are willed into existence by an eventual category winner. Let's take a look at cloud computing

---

[1] "Here's a List of 68 Bankruptcies in the Retail Apocalypse and Why They Failed." CB Insights, March 2019, https://www.cbinsights.com/research/retail-apocalypse-timeline-infographic/

technology, as an example, which has introduced innovation that has lowered the barrier to develop and ship applications at scale. The cloud has also reduced the barriers for driving customer acquisition by making it easier for customers to try and buy with models such as freemium, free trial, or pay-per-use. Today any entrepreneur with a great concept can build a technology product without a computer science degree and can become an online retailer without the need for brick and mortar. This innovation has resulted in an explosion of applications available to businesses and consumers online, pushing the software industry closer toward commoditization. If you don't believe me, Figure 4.1 illustrates the marketing technology landscape in 2019 of over 7,040 solutions as compiled by Scott Brinker and the team at the Chief Marketing Technologist blog.[2]

The impact of commoditization is typically a good thing for customers—as they now have more options than ever before when making purchasing decisions. In Chapter One, I referenced the file storage and sharing industry, which (according to G2) is a market made up of 285 vendors at the time of publishing. What's good for customers, however, is not always good for vendors operating in a crowded market—referencing the previous example, today's entrepreneurs may want to reconsider launching a new file sharing service anytime soon. Companies can choose to compete on price, but ultimately will need a more sustainable and future-proof business strategy to win market share in a crowded industry.

That's the essence of category creation, which is in effect, a response to the commoditization of industry—why join the conversation when you can just create your own? Early stage founders and marketers have the luxury of agility with positioning while being privately held, but established companies are established for a reason. They have a developed brand perception in the marketplace, are generating revenue with their core products, and in some cases have to

---

[2] Scott Brinker, "Marketing Technology Landscape Supergraphic (2019): Martech 5000 (actually 7,040)." ChiefMarTec, April 2019, https://chiefmartec .com/2019/04/marketing-technology-landscape-supergraphic-2019/

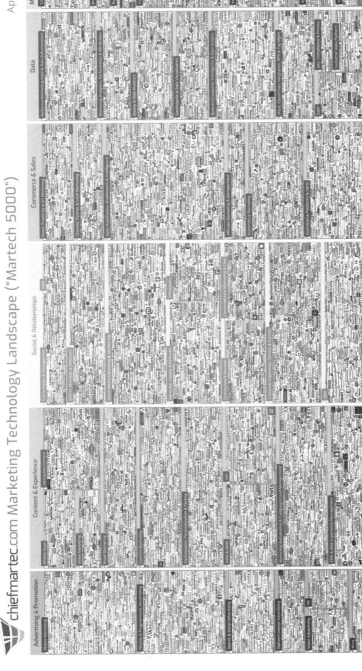

Figure 4.1   Marketing Technology Landscape Supergraphic (2019) by ChiefMarTec

answer to Wall Street for any material changes to corporate strategy. Risk aversion is indeed a real thing for enterprise brands, and the idea of creating a new market category around the core offering may seem difficult or even impossible. So what can companies in this position do to breakthrough the noise?

Option 1: Launch into a New Product Category

Established companies are typically either category incumbents (think Oracle in database technology) or fast followers who have chased and successfully challenged a market leader (think Tesla in electric cars). In either case, established companies possess a unique opportunity to uplevel their existing *market* category by launching new product offerings into entirely new *product* categories that roll into their over-arching brand promise. Product teams tasked with figuring this out will typically conduct a build, partner, buy analysis: either organically develop the new product line in house, partner with a market leader, or acquire them outright. Choosing to build comes with a unique set of challenges, including time to market and taking resources off of the core businesses. Many companies will consider partnership as a valid option to run an experiment in the new product category, the most productive of which may sometimes result in an M&A outcome. Ultimately, buying a market-leading brand and product will be the fastest path to the top position in an early market. Whichever path is chosen, launching into a new product category can often put an established company in a 1+1=3 scenario where the acquired product elevates the legacy category in new and exciting ways.

There are many examples where this has been the case—Salesforce acquired Demandware in 2016 and entered the e-commerce industry, strengthening their B2C business and expanding their customer relationship management (CRM) suite to include consumer use cases. Adobe acquired Marketo in 2018 to expand their Experience Cloud positioning to include a B2B audience. While M&A certainly isn't the only way to launch into a new product category, it's a great example of the *unfair advantage* that established brands possess over the upstart competition. Understanding how to leverage those unfair advantages, while also being aware of organizational blind spots, may be the difference between moving up the ranks and truly becoming a category leader.

Option 2: Leverage Your Unfair Advantage to Become a Category Leader

So how exactly has Best Buy managed to survive the Amazon effect and retail apocalypse? When former Best Buy CEO Hubert Joly took the position in 2012, he began to implement a series of programs that would leverage the company's unfair advantage over the competition. First, he invested in his employees, who had felt neglected under previous leadership—fixing broken internal systems, reinstating an employee discount program, and investing deeply in regular employee training. As the late Herb Kelleher, co-founder of Southwest Airlines, once said, "Employees come first. If you treat them well, then they treat the customers well, and that means your customers come back and your shareholders are happy." The adage proved true for Best Buy, who according to Glassdoor, currently boasts a 78% "recommend to a friend" rating and a 92% "approval of CEO" rating as of March 2019.

Joly understood that Best Buy's brick-and-mortar footprint was something that Amazon did not have; however, a new phenomenon called "showrooming" began to take shape in which customers would walk into a big-box store to check out a product in person before going online to buy it (cheaper) on Amazon. He viewed showrooming as an opportunity to gain advantage, given the customer was in store, and as he put it, was "ours to lose."[3] Joly instituted a price matching program and formed strategic partnerships with major electronics manufacturers such as Apple and Samsung to rent square footage

---

[3] Kevin Roose, "Best Buy's Secrets for Thriving in the Amazon Age," *New York Times*, September 2017, https://www.nytimes.com/2017/09/18/business/best-buy-amazon.html

within Best Buy's store and feature their products within a branded space. With that strategy, Amazon lost their competitive high ground on pricing, and since the customer was in store, the convenience of walking out of Best Buy with the product in-hand made more sense than waiting for an Amazon delivery.

Finally, Joly appreciated that Best Buy was able to do something that Amazon (at least for now) could not do—build relationships with customers in person. He decided to double down on services such as the *Geek Squad* technical support and the new *In-Home Advisor* programs—solutions that added value beyond the commoditized products available on the shelves, building trust and creating brand equity with the customer. While services today represent only a single-digit percentage of Best Buy's overall revenue, it's a high-margin business that's key to the company's future growth.

Best Buy will need to continue innovating to keep up with Amazon—and as a consumer, it's hard to tell whether they're on the right side of history. But Joly doesn't believe it has to be a zero-sum game, saying, "You won't get me to say a bad word about Amazon. There is a lot of room for both of us."[4]

In Best Buy's case, they were able to leverage these unfair advantages—their engaged workforce, physical footprint, customer relationships, and value-added services—to break away from the noise in their industry and build a new type of retail experience with customers at the center. There are common unfair advantages that established brands possess over the competition that can be extremely helpful levers to reposition away from a crowded marketplace. While established brands are often given a bad rep (slow and inefficient) relative to nimble and innovative startups, these same weaknesses can be turned into strengths in order to accelerate market dominance at a pace no startup could ever compete with. Here are three common unfair advantages to consider leveraging.

---

[4] Justin Bariso, "Amazon Almost Killed Best Buy. Then, Best Buy Did Something Completely Brilliant." *Inc.*, September 2017, https://www.inc.com/justin-bariso /amazon-almost-killed-best-buy-then-best-buy-did-something-completely -brilliant.html

1. Existing Customer Base

The very definition of established brand connotes an active install base of customers who are already using your products or services. The relationships that have been developed with customers over the years will serve as a strategic advantage over competition still focused on acquiring an initial set of early adopters. Customers can serve as invaluable sources of feedback on positioning through programs such as *customer advisory boards* or *brand advocates* willing to evangelize in the marketplace. If you're considering launching a new product offering to the same buyer as your core business, your customers are the highest leveraged demand gen expense as you aim to cross-sell the new product offering. If the new product offering is targeting a completely different buyer, customers are (again) a high-leverage referral source for introductions to the new buyer at the customer account.

In either case, established brands can leverage the laws of price elasticity to launch new offerings into their installed base in clever ways. Imagine a promotion to existing customers where they can access the new product offering for free (or cheap) for one year, so long as they agree to fully evaluate your solution as a rip-and-replace of what they're currently using at the time of renewal. In this example, the barrier to entry for customers is pretty low (no cost), demonstrates value (product capabilities), and the costs to acquire a customer are much lower than programs at the top of the funnel. Perhaps customers who participate will also agree to serve as early advocates of the new product line—providing a quote, rights to use their logo publicly, or even participating in marketing programs such as webinars and live events. Developing the competitive offer is easy (meaning any company can technically do that), but the hard thing is developing an engaged customer base to launch into—an unfair advantage that only established companies possess.

2. Established Brand Equity

While startup companies find themselves in a position where they need to build their brands from the ground up, established companies have already done so. As an example, when you see the Ford logo, you have a cognitive reference embedded in your mind of a generational American company that has transformed the transportation industry. As Ford builds, partners, or buys their way into bike share programs, commuter shuttle services, or even electric scooters, the company can lean on the brand equity that it has developed in the marketplace as the transportation and mobility leader to extend that very leadership into emerging business lines. A startup in the electric scooter industry has to work exponentially harder to win the trust of consumers.

It's also critically important for established companies to be continually evolving while never compromising their purpose, promise, and values. Warren Buffet's adage that "it takes 20 years to build a reputation and five minutes to ruin it" is especially relevant in this context. However, marketing itself is in a constant state of renewal, and established brands need to leverage emerging communications mediums to stay relevant to their evolving customer base. You can think of several examples in the consumer world of companies who have been able to leverage their tenured brand equity while also keeping up with modern marketing practices—Coca-Cola, Disney, and Nike, just to name a few. The chapters that follow will offer exciting ideas to strengthen established brand equity in engaging and relevant ways.

3. Budget and Go-to-Market (GTM) Resources

Recall that one of the six challenges to creating a category that I referenced in the last chapter was having enough capital deployed to create a broad level of awareness around unmet need in the marketplace. This is especially difficult for bootstrapped startups, but not always the case for established companies making a conscious effort to invest. There are several budget levers that give advantage to established companies over startup competition:

- **Program Budget.** Marketers can spend money to buy their way into new markets through paid media, creating organic content optimized for long-tail search, exhibiting at industry tradeshows, and so on. The less resources are constrained, the fewer tradeoffs have to be made on which programs marketing can invest in to grow awareness in the early innings.

- **Headcount.** Especially in early markets, established brands have an opportunity to scale hiring sales reps, content marketers, and other GTM functions in order to overwhelm the capacity of startups.

- **M&A.** As I mentioned earlier, a thoughtful business case on new market entry will typically include a build, partner, or buy analysis—where companies are faced with a decision on whether to pursue organic product development, strategic partnerships, or M&A in order to launch into new categories. Acquiring a company may prove to be the fastest path to entering a new market in a leadership position.

Budget and resources are critical advantages for established brands that can enable faster path to market leadership; however, accessing the dollars alone will not create the advantage. One edge that startups gain from the absence of resources is the requirement to be conservative with spend, test assumptions before making big bets, and ultimately prove the ROI of each dollar spent in sales and marketing. The playbook that I'll share in the chapters that follow will give you and your teams the tools they need to execute on either of the above two approaches with more resources than our startup friends, but with the same degree of innovation and creativity.

PART

II

Seven Principles to Create (and Dominate) a Category

5

Live Your Purpose, Values, and Culture Out Loud

We've all seen the TED talk by now. At the time of writing this, Simon Sinek's 18-minute monologue on how great leaders inspire action has drawn almost 44 million views and has secured its place as one of the top 25 most popular TED talks of all time. Sinek's message was as profound as it was simple—that people don't buy *what* you do; they buy *why* you do it. The greatest generational companies of our time, such as Apple, Harley-Davidson, and Southwest Airlines, deliver so much more than just products customers love; they create movements around their brands. Their secret? According to Sinek, these outlier companies inspire loyalty and motivate their followers and employees to stick with them through thick or thin by starting with *why*, while their competitors start with *what*.

Category creation, too, must start with *why*.

The truth is that every company—whether creating a new category or disrupting an existing one—should define their purpose and what they stand for as an organization. Purpose is foundational to success in the B2H era. With products (the *what*) becoming more commoditized over time, customers have more choice than ever before and will elect to do business with companies they respect and admire. Aligning brand to core human need has become far more than just the right thing to do, but the only way for a company to survive. This is especially true of companies creating a category, which, as I explained in Chapter One, is a noble mission that requires the patience of long-term greed in order to inspire an entire market into existence. Inspiration becomes a "higher calling" for both employees enrolled in the mission and members of the community who participate. To be successful in this endeavor, your brand *must* stand for something bigger than simply the products that you create, and beyond that, the community needs to know it.

There are several reasons why living your purpose out loud is the foundation of creating and dominating a new category. Purpose informs your brand, shows the industry and community a preview of the world you are creating, and inspires the values that will guide your decision making along the journey. Purpose draws talent into your company, retaining leaders within the movement that you're building and creating a sense of vocational fulfillment through seasons of both triumph and trial. Purpose inspires your community to navigate uncharted waters together toward the idealistic true north that you've described. Finally, purpose helps grow your business by attracting customers who build stronger emotional connections that go far beyond a transactional relationship. According to the *2018 Cone/Porter Novelli Purpose Study*, nearly eight in ten (79%) of Americans say they are more loyal to purpose-driven brands than to traditional brands and 66% would switch from a product they typically buy, to a new product from a purpose-driven company.[1]

A great example of a modern, purpose-driven brand in B2B is ServiceNow, the leading digital workflow company who in 2018 went through an exercise to dial into their purpose. They also just happen to be the second most valuable cloud company in the world, with a $50B+ market cap—no coincidence there. ServiceNow was founded by Fred Luddy in 2004 on a simple idea of helping everyday people route work across the enterprise—a mantra that gave the company and their employees deep meaning in creating technology in the service of people. They arrived at a re-articulation

---

[1] "2018 Cone/Porter Novelli Purpose Study: How to Build Deeper Bonds, Amplify Your Message and Expand the Consumer Base," Cone/Porter Novelli, 2018, http://www.conecomm.com/research-blog/2018-purpose-study

servicenow·   servicenow.

Figure 5.1   ServiceNow Brand Identity Past and Present

of their purpose in 2018 of "we make work, work better for people," a powerful statement that remains true to Luddy's original vision for the company and thrust ServiceNow deep into the heart of the future of work conversation. Dan Rogers, chief marketing officer at ServiceNow, referred to the process they took to articulate purpose as "a grounding effort for the whole company" and at the core of "everything [they] do." Purpose serves as a source of inspiration for ServiceNow's employees, who work for a company with a *why* that they themselves can connect to personally.

ServiceNow debuted their refreshed purpose at their Knowledge conference in May 2018 before a captive audience of 18,000 attendees. Part of the announcement included the reveal of their refreshed brand expression that featured a new corporate identity, as seen in Figure 5.1. The company brilliantly expressed their purpose in the visual design of the logo itself, choosing to move away from the product-centric on/off visual in the "o" of the logo to a human-centric person icon. As Rogers put it, the notion "that you could find yourself in our logo is a very important idea for us." For Rogers and the ServiceNow team, purpose was not merely a clever line of marketing copy written on the homepage, but the rudder for how the company operates and how it shows up and expresses itself in the marketplace. They believe it deeply, but they also live it out loud.

How to Develop a Shared Vision Around Company Purpose

One of the most prolific voices on the power of purpose in building enduring companies is Jim Collins, an author, consultant, and lecturer who has written six books that have sold more than 10 million copies in total worldwide. In perhaps his most iconic work, *Built to Last: Successful Habits of Visionary Companies,* Collins drew upon a

six-year research project at Stanford University of 18 truly exceptional and generational companies that have an average age of nearly
100 years and have outperformed the general stock market by a factor
of 15 since 1926. One of the key reasons why these companies have
withstood the test of time is an early orientation around defining
what Collins calls *core ideology* in both purpose and values. In *Built to
Last*, Collins goes on to name five important characteristics of a good
expression of a company's core purpose:

1. It absolutely has to be inspiring to those *inside* the company.
2. It has to be something that could be as valid 100 years from
   now as it is today.
3. It should help you think expansively about what you *could* do
   but aren't doing.
4. It should help you decide what *not* to do.
5. It has to be truly authentic to your company.

Disney's purpose is to "make people happy"—a timeless statement that checks the box for all five principles. Southwest Airlines'
purpose, similarly, is to "democratize the skies." The sentiment of
Collins's five principles were reflected in a 1960 speech by David
Packard to Hewlett-Packard's training group, where he said, "purpose should not be confused with specific goals or business strategies (which should change many times in 100 years). Whereas you
might achieve a goal or complete a strategy, you cannot fulfill a
purpose; it's like a guiding star on the horizon—forever pursued but
never reached. Yet although purpose itself does not change, it does
inspire change. The very fact that purpose can never be fully realized means that an organization can never stop stimulating change
and progress."

Arriving at shared organizational purpose may feel like an
intimidating endeavor since companies are made up of diverse sets
of individuals, and purpose, by its very nature, is an emotional and
often personal construct. In order to help demystify the process, I've
recruited the help of John Rex, the former CFO of Microsoft North

America, whose firm, Rex Executive Leadership, is a leading source of leadership coaching for technology executives. John helps growth-minded executives deliver impact and accelerate their success and believes great leadership is grounded in humility. Inspired by Jim Collins and his five principles of company purpose, John believes that there are three important steps that you and your teams can take to put those principles into action and articulate your very own purpose:

1. **Start by Defining the Individual Purpose of the Executive Team.** The truth is that whether you start here explicitly or otherwise, company purpose will *always* correlate to personal purpose. The two components of expressing personal purpose are defining (a) your talents, gifts, or core competencies and (b) how you choose to employ those gifts out in the world. As executive teams set out to answer those two questions and artic- ulate their own higher purpose, the outcome of that discovery will almost certainly result in an expression like the following: *I want to get better as a human, and in the process of doing so, I want to lift up others and help them achieve what's important to them.* This personal expression of purpose is completely analogous to insti- tutional purpose—most companies will strive to change the world, self-actualize in their careers, and drive business results (get better as humans), while also providing customers with value to do the same (lift up others). Open discussion among the executive team on what each individual's purpose is can lead to insightful areas of overlap. Leaders will employ their talents, gifts, and core competencies—a bundle unique to each individual—in an effort to fulfill their purpose, whether per- sonal or corporate. John's research has found that a conscious effort of starting with individual purpose in order to articulate corporate purpose leads to much more effective outcomes.

2. **Break Out in Small Groups to Look for the Golden Threads.** Engaging in conversation around the individual purpose(s) of the executive team can set the stage for a collective discovery process on how personal purpose informs

corporate purpose. Ask each other questions like: What business are we *really* in? What is the benefit of our service to our customers and society at large? Why does that matter? What is the end result we offer? Why does that matter? Why do we exist? Golden threads will start to emerge in the conversation around these questions, and sooner or later, the group will rally around a definition of purpose that both strikes an emotional chord and becomes deeply meaningful as a reflection of the individual purpose represented in the room. Memorialize that definition as your company purpose, recognizing that the best purpose statements are centered around why you are going to help your customers achieve what matters most to them.

3. **Develop a People Strategy Informed by Shared Institutional Purpose.** Building a company means bringing together a unique set of individuals to execute an extraordinary vision— one that we've described for category creators as a noble mission. Companies must provide this diverse set of voices, experiences, and talents with a vessel by which they can live out their personal values and purpose in a way that accomplishes the mission of the institution. That's where the purpose statement articulated in the second step comes in—a container that becomes a filter for how organizations recruit, enable, and align teams in the pursuit of institutional purpose. Amazon is an example of a company made up of individuals who refer to the corporate purpose and leadership principles every single day. The Amazon purpose is operationalized into their people strategy—whether in recruiting or performance reviews. Amazon realizes that purpose can't just be lip service or a statement on a website, but the most important component of how to build and lead organizations of people.

Setting aside time with your team to develop and articulate purpose is an important exercise to understanding why your company exists, and the role you'll play in creating a category. There are also benefits to hiring professional facilitators like John to assist in this discovery process—whether to help overcome the bias of agreeing with the boss or to enable the group to do their best thinking without the distraction of orchestrating conversation.

Also, defining the *why* behind your business is only the beginning of truly unlocking the leadership principles that will power your success moving forward. Leadership coaches can help teams build on their purpose by articulating vision (who they want to become), values (how they choose to act), and operating principles (the way things get done in alignment with purpose, vision, and values). While making the time and resources available for this discovery process can be misconstrued as a distraction, make no mistake, it's ultimately the foundation of your success in category creation.

At Gainsight, we've always been extremely values-driven as a company, even from day one. Today our values point back to our shared purpose and are used to help ensure that each of our teammates, from leadership to early career, are always working in alignment toward the same goal. But I will admit, we approached the effort a bit out of order—starting with the *how* over the *why*. From the early days of the company, we knew that we wanted to build a company that behaved in accordance with the following principles:

- **Golden Rule.** Treat people the way you'd like to be treated.
- **Success for All.** Our "bottom line" requires us to drive success for not only shareholders, but also customers, teammates, their families, and our communities around us.
- **Childlike Joy.** Bring the kid in you to work every day.
- **Shoshin.** Cultivate a "Beginner's Mind."
- **Stay Thirsty, My Friends.** Have ambition that comes from within.

Our values were always deeply meaningful for us, but alone, lacked an expression into a deeper purpose of our daily effort building enterprise software. Don't get me wrong; there's a lot of good in enterprise software, but we're not exactly trying to save humanity by flying rockets and cars into space to one day colonize new worlds (thanks for setting the bar, Elon). If your job, like mine, is doing something that you think is important but isn't quite in the category of "the future of human existence," how do you justify it to yourself and your team? Enterprise software can certainly be a good business, but can it feel good too?

One day it hit us, that we may not change the world with what we do, in a realistic sense, but we can change the worlds of those around us in terms of *why* and *how* we do the things we do. We long for something different in the *why* and the *how* of business. We respect the bottom line and recognize its importance, but we don't bow down to it as our only master. People are just as important as business—and they aren't "assets" or "human capital," as some companies might claim. Not everything has to drive to shareholder value, because you can have multiple goals. Teammates can thrive at work without having to give themselves up in the process. In fact, we believe society needs this more than ever.

With artificial intelligence, automation, robots, and the like, humans are having our own existential crisis. Every screen, selfie, and social network makes us long that much more for a real smile and shared moment. So we finally wrote it down. We decided on the *why* that would keep us going long beyond the day-to-day. Our purpose at Gainsight is: *to be living proof that you can win in business while being human-first.*

Human-first means always thinking about people in the decisions you make about business:

- Human-first means realizing that the life and time of the person running your office and that of the person cleaning your office are equally important and valuable.
- Human-first means being radically transparent with your team—even when it feels uncomfortable.
- Human-first means making sure that the company's schedule and work/collaboration environment are flexible so your team can make the piano recital, friends' night out, or family trip.
- Human-first means welcoming every teammate as though he or she is the most important person in the company—because they all are!

- Human-first means congratulating and celebrating a teammate who is leaving for the next dream job versus treating him like a traitor or trying to make him feel guilty.
- Human-first means thinking about your competition not as evil or bad, but rather as a bunch of people just as good as you are trying to live their lives and support their families.
- Human-first means leadership, including CEOs, opening up to their teams and to the world about their brightest dreams and their darkest fears.

Does human-first mean you don't make tough decisions? Of course not. Human-first companies will do things from time to time that don't feel great. But our test for Gainsight is that if we're causing pain for others in the interest of a "rational" decision, we better be feeling that pain ourselves many times over—or we've lost our humanity. That pain is what will make us always think of people in decision making. We feel like we can help a lot of humans—between our customers, our teammates, their families, our shareholders, and our communities. Maybe it's not all of humanity, but it's a start. And if we, like many other companies going down this path, can help other businesses open their eyes to another way to work, that impact can grow even more.

The Power of Purpose in Category Creation

For companies like Gainsight that are creating new categories, there's a hyper-important sixth characteristic that did not make it onto Collins's classic list from 1994—*it absolutely must be inspiring to your community as well.* Call it the Kennada Amendment, but the whole notion of cultivating a tribe of people who are bound together by common purpose is as powerful in the professional context as it is influential in our social psychology as humans. This is especially the case in new markets, as individual early adopters can often feel like they're on their career journey alone. We'll unpack why building and growing community is key to category creation in Chapter Eight, but the truth is that any community or tribe of people will look to a leader to guide them into the future—an imperative for any brand desiring a market leadership position. Earning that title requires creating and articulating an inspirational purpose for the company in service of the community, and being able to build good habits to activate that purpose and truly live it out loud. If executed correctly, communities will actually reflect the culture of the market leader, creating an emotional connection between the two parties.

In a recursive sort of way, Gainsight's purpose nests well in the purpose of the customer success community—the movement that we serve at Gainsight. Customer success is fundamentally about realizing that your customer is not a transaction or a deal or an opportunity or a lead. Your customer is a bunch of human beings just like you. And just like you, they want to succeed with what they do. In a way, customer success is about bringing humanity back into this technology-driven world. We revealed our new human-first purpose on stage at our Pulse 2018 conference in front of over 5,000 members of our community who adopted the phrase as a rallying cry of their own. They've always known that customer success is fundamentally a human endeavor, but we put that intuition into words and invested to activate them in the marketplace—giving all who would listen an opportunity to join the movement we were building.

How to Activate Purpose and Values

Once you've arrived at a shared organizational purpose, your job is far from over. Like the ServiceNow and Gainsight examples from earlier in the chapter demonstrated, your purpose needs to create resonance outside the walls of your organization and into the community that you're creating. Marketing plays a critical role here to "activate" purpose, or said another way, to increase both internal and external awareness and engagement around it. That's critically important to make sure everyone who interacts with your brand—whether online, in meetings, or at live events—can be left with an impression of who you are and what you stand for. These activations, when communicated authentically, help invest in your brand equity as the category leader and inspire your followers to stay engaged as you lead them into the future. Here are a few ideas for ways marketers can activate purpose into the marketplace:

- Explain your purpose and values on the company page of your website, describing why you chose them and what they mean to you. This is effectively the "front door" of who you are as an organization and what you stand for. Don't make this page static or an afterthought.
- Produce blog posts and other forms of content that can be shared in order to inspire your audience at scale. While these content assets may be less focused on your category or your products, they become powerful representations of what you stand for that can create a halo effect around your brand.
- Include a standard slide in sales decks or any other presentations in order to inject purpose and values into your corporate narrative. The audience on the other end of the presentation will appreciate a deeper understanding of who you are and how you see the world.
- Create a platform for your executive team to express a personal point of view as the face of the brand and community. The market will look to the leadership teams behind category creators as representatives of the brand's purpose and values. Chapter Eleven is dedicated to this topic and will provide specific tactics for building an authentic executive communications strategy.
- Leverage PR to provide sound bites and comments in the media on conversations relevant to your purpose. Journalists use a service called HARO (Help a Reporter Out) to find sources for upcoming stories and daily opportunities for sources to secure valuable media coverage. That's an easy—albeit reactive—strategy for brands to lead with purpose in highly visible channels.

- Talk about purpose and values on stage at industry conferences, while activating your own event production efforts as expressions of the same. As an example of the latter point, if one of your company values is focused on diversity or equality for all stakeholders, what measures will your event team take to ensure equal representation on stage and in the audience?

These are only a few ideas to start activating your purpose and values—concepts that when developed authentically, can create a halo effect around your brand in the early market you are building and leading. As you add other ideas to the list, you'll notice a dedicated track starting to emerge within your content marketing strategy that's focused on purpose and corporate marketing. Your audience will continue to have an interest that goes well beyond *what* you're doing to build your category, but *how*, and most importantly, *why*. But external members of your community are not the only ones paying attention to these activations. It's important to keep purpose and values in front of teammates as well, as they, ultimately, are the most important constituents of these principles and whose buy-in may be the difference between success and failure in the long game of category creation.

Why Purpose, Values, and Culture Matter to Teammates

I mentioned earlier that category creation carries a "higher calling" for both members of the community as well as for teammates who are enrolled in the mission. Defining an inspiring core ideology is the most powerful way to recruit talent into your company and retain them for the long (and I mean *long*) road ahead. As leaders of companies, it's important to think about teammates as our internal customers. Like the trends we're seeing with clients in the marketplace, employees today have more choices than ever before of companies they can work for. Activating your purpose in the marketplace can become a competitive advantage for talent recruitment that differentiates your brand from other "disruptors" in the industry.

Also, the reality is that category creation, as we discussed in Chapter Three, can be *extremely* difficult. While other companies may enjoy obvious product/market fit in a category that is well established, category creators must invent both product and market at the same time. Figuring out repeatable sales models and scalable GTM processes will come over time and typically after making many mistakes—a convicting purpose and set of values can keep the team engaged and pushing through, create deep meaning in their work, and focus on the noble mission at hand. A 2014 survey from the Energy Project, an engagement and performance firm that focuses on workplace fulfillment, found that 50% of employees lack a level of meaning and significance at work. However, employees who derive meaning from their work are more than three times as likely to stay with their company, and also report 1.7x higher job satisfaction and are 1.4x more engaged at work.[2]

Defining the *why* behind your company is the critical first step of your category creation journey that will inform the rest of your decision making going forward. But now that you've started with *why*, it's time to focus on the *who*.

---

[2] Jessica Amortegui, "Why Finding Meaning at Work Is More Important Than Feeling Happy," *Fast Company*, June 26, 2014, https://www.fastcompany.com/3032126/how-to-find-meaning-during-your-pursuit-of-happiness-at-work

6 | Focus on the People in Your Market— Not Just Your Products

How can we learn to be great at something? A few generations ago, the answer might have been to read about the craft at the local library or apprentice under a recognized expert. In the Internet age, a simple web search or *"Hey, Siri"* can lead to a limitless spring of information and education—how-to videos, detailed blog posts, or even following business luminaries on social media. Consumers today are learning new languages online, sharing recipes on international cuisines, and even graduating from accredited universities, all from the comfort of their laptops, tablets, and mobile devices. This desire to realize our fullest potential as humans is, according to American psychologist Abraham Maslow, our highest motivation for psychological health once our most basic needs (such as physical survival, safety, and others) are met. Aiding in our efforts towards self-actualization is the abundance of educational content available online on quite literally any topic, whether professionally created, community/user generated, or otherwise.

As we discussed in Chapter Two, category creation is in and of itself a subset of B2H marketing—a belief that behind every logo that companies are trying to market and sell to is a human, somewhere on

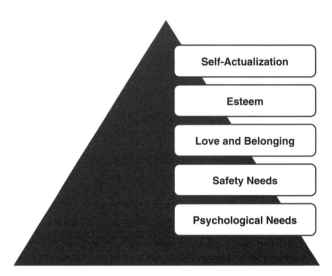

Figure 6.1 Maslow's Hierarchy of Needs Pyramid

Maslow's pyramid and hierarchy of needs (see Figure 6.1 as a reference). Unique to category creation is the realization that no company in the world is paying attention to that particular human (or set of humans) in a meaningful way, or at least in the context of their quest to solve this particular problem that you've observed for the first time. Your job in defining the category, at a very simplistic level, is to serve them as a trusted advisor on their journey up the pyramid. Can you help them justify the strategic importance of their role or initiative within the organization to management (safety)? Can you build a community of peers and innovators around them (belonging)? Can you help them get promoted or recognized at their company and within the industry (esteem)? These are some of the most basic needs within early markets that are unmet and typically have little *direct* correlation to your products and services. Focusing marketing efforts here will make the difference between success and failure in category creation.

People are at the heart of category creation, not products. I mentioned in Chapter One that one of the signals that there may be a category to create is the existence of a passionate niche of people who "get it" set within a larger population of people who don't.

These early adopters are people who understand the pain and believe that you're onto something, even if investors, analysts, and others do not. Eventually your products will matter to them, especially if positioned as an accelerator to movement up Maslow's pyramid. However, through the filter of business-to-human, developing a content marketing strategy that speaks to all levels of the pyramid can build that trusted advisorship and category leadership that's much more impactful than positioning feature benefit in the early innings of new markets. People care about their careers, but careers, in the broadest sense, can mean so much more than just work. How are you building the foundations of your category to support the people within it?

The Psychology of Early Adopters in New Categories

New categories tend to attract a certain type of person—a pioneering spirit known as an "early adopter." The term was first introduced by American communication theorist and sociologist Everett Rogers in his 1962 book *Diffusion of Innovations*, a landmark effort that has become the foundation for modern thinking about how ideas and products spread. Rogers defines early adopters as influencers early in the innovation adoption lifecycle (see Figure 6.2) who test new products and ideas and become the influencers who drive subsequent phases of adoption. If this sounds familiar, you'll certainly recognize

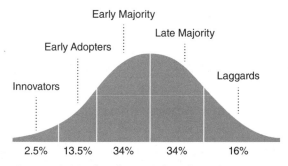

Figure 6.2   Rogers's Technology Adoption Curve

the line between early adopter and early majority as the toughest leap of the entire curve and representative of the "chasm" popularized by Geoffrey Moore's *Crossing the Chasm: Marketing and Selling Disruptive Products to Mainstream Customers.* But before the chasm can even come into view, you'll have to understand what drives early adopters, whose validation is a prerequisite for spreading new ideas into the mainstream.

Early adopters are subject to the same observations of Abraham Maslow in his hierarchy of needs theory. The primary differences are the psychological drivers underlying their progress toward self-actualization—motivations that Forrester Research identifies as information, novelty, and status.[1] Early adopters are diligent researchers who have set themselves up to learn about new things before anyone else, thus underscoring the requirement for aspiring category creators to saturate the web with content regarding the problem your category addresses. Early adopters tend to jump on board to new ideas earlier than most, but that risk is mitigated by the research they've done before throwing their support behind a concept. These folks are also driven by novelty or, said another way, the success and competitive advantage that can be realized by adopting a trend early and ahead of the market. According to the Forrester Research survey, early adopters are 72% more likely to say: "I am always willing to try and do new things" than the "laggards" at the right end of the bell curve. The third motivator for early adopters is status, or choosing to affiliate (or be the novel first to affiliate) with brands that represent them in the world. From a professional context, early adopters care deeply about their personal brands and will respond favorably to companies who engage them in opportunities to build or promote themselves.

Creating a category will require building a groundswell of support from early adopters in the industry—the select few who already "get it" and those within their sphere of influence. Understanding how to

---

[1] Abe Garon and James McQuivey, "The Psychology of Early Adopters," Forrester Research, November 2009, https://www.forrester.com/report/The+Psychology+Of+Early+Adopters/-/E-RES55614

develop content, community, and other strategies that activate their motivations of information, novelty, and status is critical. Whether that's telling their story on your blog as innovators in the category, providing them with speaking opportunities, or asking them to speak on a podcast, getting early adopters on your team early is important to build long-term brand equity in the category. Their support can create a network effect that propels category awareness and thought leadership into the marketplace, sparking a flywheel that will compound and gain momentum as time goes on. We'll cover these tactics throughout the course of the book, but regardless of how the narrative is presented (live events, digital, otherwise), at the heart of the strategy is building a content marketing machine with early adopters in mind.

A Primer on Content Marketing

Starting and scaling a content marketing engine may sound daunting: Who will do the writing? How do we distribute? and How exactly do we find time for all of this anyway? That's what this chapter is all about, whether you're starting from scratch or looking to reimagine your content efforts through the lens of category creation. However, before we dive in, I'd like to define some basic language around content marketing—definitions and key considerations that I learned early in my time at Gainsight from Marketo who (along with others) evangelized this era of content marketing. Content marketing, as Marketo defines it, "is the process of creating high-quality, valuable content to attract, inform, and engage an audience, while also promoting the brand itself."[2] They go on to classify different types of content into three buckets: early stage, middle stage, and late stage content.

- **Early Stage Content.** Content positioned pre-purchase or during the "awareness" stage of the buyer's journey. This is typically referred to as "thought leadership" content meant to

---

[2] "Content Marketing," Marketo, https://www.marketo.com/content-marketing/

educate while building brand awareness. Sample form factors include blogs, e-books, research data, infographics, and webinars and they are most often not gated (or locked behind a web form).

- **Middle Stage Content.** Tools that help buyers find you when they are in the market for a product or solution during the "consideration" stage of the buyer's journey. Typical form factors include buying guides, RFP templates, ROI calculators, and analyst reports. Middle stage content is almost always gated in order to capture the buying intent and route leads appropriately to the sales team for follow-up.
- **Late Stage Content.** Content made available during the "evaluation" stage of the buyer's journey to help buyers evaluate and reaffirm their selection of your company. Typical form factors include pricing, services, on-boarding information, and customer case studies. Late stage content is typically not gated and will often be best leveraged to enable the sales team to advance their pipeline and close deals.

In category creation, the majority of effort and resources are spent developing early stage content, educating the market on a problem they don't know they have, why it's important, and how to solve it. Figure 6.3 gives a few examples of early stage content themes

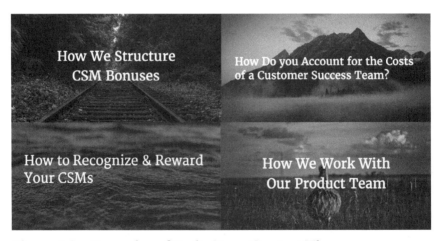

Figure 6.3   Examples of Early Stage Content Themes

that we've published at Gainsight. It's critical that the narrative is early-stage in nature, and even more critical that the content is delivered by you as the aspirational category leader. Not only will early stage content efforts build thought leadership equity for your brand, but since the nature of the subject is educational rather than promotional, these assets are indexed by search engines and will eventually drive considerable organic traffic to your website, fueling your inbound marketing machine. More than six years into Gainsight, there are still content assets online that were originally written in 2013 that are performing great and driving inbound lead velocity for us. Today over 60% of the traffic to Gainsight.com is through organic channels, a testament to the early stage content marketing investments we've made from early days and continue to invest in today.

So what do you do with middle and late stage content in new categories? These types of assets are important to develop, just not quite as important as early stage content in the foundational chapters of your journey. As your category starts to mature, middle and late stage content assets are critical to position your solution as the answer of record to the problem that the market is now starting to understand. However, successfully executing an early stage content marketing strategy does not come without its challenges, mainly the *two funnel effect* that I introduced in Chapter Three. In the two funnel effect, you become extremely successful in driving broad awareness of your market and category (funnel one), but struggle to monetize that brand impact into closed revenue of your product or service (funnel two).

One of the ways to build a bridge from funnel one to funnel two, or to otherwise inspire a product evaluation within your new category, is to take middle and late stage content, remove them from behind the gate, and promote them as if they were early stage content. The idea here is to teach your market how to buy products and solutions for the problem they've uncovered, as it's often the case that new categories do not have universally understood sales processes. Consider creating a *Platform Buyer's Guide* e-book and promoting that on social media or to your marketable database. Invest early in customer testimonials and case studies—a strategy we'll cover in depth in Chapter Nine—and drive widespread awareness and engagement around that content. Design a sample RFP asset and promote that to your audience, evangelizing buying criteria for products in your new category. Classic content marketing guidelines would suggest most of this content ought to live behind a gate or content management system that your sales team alone can access, but putting some promotional muscle behind middle and late stage content can help build a bridge between awareness and consideration within your new category. Before we get too far down that road, however, let's discuss how to develop a content marketing strategy in the first place.

Developing a Content Marketing Strategy for New Categories

Whether you're building a content strategy from the ground up or are interested in revisiting your existing programs through the lens of category creation, there are five principles you'll need to keep in mind.

1. Name Your Category

One of the most significant decisions early in the category creation journey is what to name your category. Identifying a category name will do more than just unite your company, but also serve as a rallying call for the entire community of prospects and customers within your market. You're going to be spending a lot of time and resources creating content around the category name, betting a non-trivial amount of marketing budget that your choice category is a massive, multi-billion-dollar market worthy of attention. Deciding on the name isn't necessarily easy, as analysts won't recognize it (more on that in Chapter Ten), competition will call it something else, tangential categories already exist and are causing confusion, search volume is extremely low for most of your ideas, and all the good domains are already taken. Sound familiar?

Although there aren't a lot of universal truths on how to come up with a category name, here are a few tips that can guide your thinking:

- **Brand around people, not the product.** Analysts have a habit of coming up with extremely complex category names devoid of any human emotion that also happen to make great acronyms. Enterprise Content Management (ECM), Recurring Revenue Management (RRM), or Security Information and Event Management (SIEM) are just a few examples. Consider instead anchoring your category name on the outcomes that your customers hope to achieve through your products.
- **Look for clues in customer job titles.** Consider the job titles of your prospective customers and create a connection with what's unique in your category. At Gainsight we discovered that a role had already existed and predated us called the *Customer Success Manager,* but no company was creating any content around Customer Success. It seemed like a good option for us to consider.
- **Use Google Trends to gauge search volume.** Search volume will inherently be low for a new category—if not, I would question how new the proposed category actually is. But by using Google Trends, you're able to quantify the little traffic that is being driven to your short list of category names. The data gives you a small window into interest and search behavior of the broad market—best served as a way to benchmark your best ideas against your worst.

Selecting a category name is the first step of your content marketing journey. Once you get there, wave the flag for the category everywhere you possibly can—buy the domains, write to the hashtag, set up social analytics and Google Alerts to track share of voice and search volume. Since you'll be committing to creating momentum for the category brand, benchmarking what the world looked like the day you named it is not a bad idea. Now all that's left to do is a whole lot of writing—so who's going to do it all?

2. Identify Spokespeople, Writers, and Contributors

Figuring out where all this content is expected to come from can be a difficult proposition. In the early days of category creation, it's entirely possible that all of the subject matter expertise is trapped inside the head of the founder or chief executive and difficult to transfer over to a junior marketer or agency. Later on, as a company matures, the target executive or department within your organization (e.g., CMO/Marketing at HubSpot or CRO/Sales at Salesforce) can be a great source of content contribution. Some companies have even hired subject matter experts who are early adopters in the young market as *evangelists* who write content and speak at events as their full-time job. Regardless of who does the actual writing, it's important to identify who within the company will serve as the external spokesperson and provide that name on the byline of the articles written.

In order to do the actual writing, hiring a content writer as one of the first few employees in Marketing is a good idea. Writers can either develop a piece of content based on a recorded interview or outline or edit content provided by a founder or executive. Writers can also capture your *brand voice* and ensure that all assets are in compliance before publishing to the web. Since the nature of the content is early stage, a great way to scale your content program while tapping into the status motivator of the early adopters in your market is to ask customers (or non-customer members of your community) to contribute content as well. Not having every article on your web properties written by someone at your company has a positive secondary effect on your credibility as the category leader.

Content Hack for Early Stage Startups

I have the privilege of meeting with early stage founders who are interested in category creation, but are still extremely early in their operations and have no marketers on staff. I explain to them how important content marketing is to the strategy, and every time, I can physically see the reality of scarce resources set in over them. We are very fortunate at Gainsight to have a CEO who loves to write. In the early days before in-flight Wi-Fi was widespread, we used to joke that we can send Nick on a cross-country flight (without Internet) and he'd land having sent us three to five complete blog posts.

Although that might sound silly, there's actually something profound hidden in that story. As I mentioned earlier, the vision for a new category and its unique positioning are often locked in the minds of the founding team. Since both time and resources are scarce, I've advised founders to commit to one weekend of writing—perhaps with no Wi-Fi—to create 12 chapters of an e-book manifesto for the new category. Twelve chapters is strategic, as each topic could become a monthly theme for a campaign: blog post, webinar, sales dinner topic, and so on. Working with partners to write response articles for each of the 12 will add some much needed validation early in your efforts, and if launched together, could build your marketable database by leveraging their audiences as well. All you need is one weekend to write and you'll leave with an entire year of content.

3. Articulate the "Why" Behind Your Category

Remember that the very definition of category creation assumes that no one has been able to observe or articulate the problem that you've discovered in the market. That's the initial focus of your content marketing efforts—proving the existence of the problem and making the case for why a new category has taken shape to address it. Third-party anecdotes and supporting voices may be helpful in validating your position. If successful, you'll be able to convince the early adopters in your market that there's something novel here worth paying attention to and that there's a company out there who understands what they're going through.

You'll have to do more than just speak their language, however. As Maslow's pyramid would indicate, humans have a psychological need for safety that may be triggered before they can bet their careers on your category positioning. Create content that helps the newly converted justify an investment in your category to their executives and networks. Arm them with the data, case studies, and other proof points that they need to create broad awareness inside and outside of their organization in order to green light a project. We've spent a lot of time at Gainsight writing content on how to justify an investment in Customer Success to the CEO or board. We also created a business case for Customer Success by quantifying the pain of churn through an ROI study conducted through a third-party research firm (as referenced in Chapter Three). Assets like these helped us prove to the world that churn was a problem for subscription companies and that Customer Success was the appropriate strategy to address it.

4. Educate on the "How"

After getting some momentum behind your category, the logical next set of questions from people in the young community will be around *how* to actually put the learnings of the category into practice. The market will naturally look to you as the company evangelizing the category for resources on best practices—an expectation that will frankly never go away. Build the online destination for category best practices on your blog, so that the market will come to align your website with industry thought leadership. Beyond the associated brand benefit, the content hosted on your blog will create a long tail of thought leadership indexed across search engines, driving organic traffic to your site when published with SEO considerations. In fact, a good way to think about your blog is as a publishing platform for your category—any early adopters in the community who have a story to tell should desire to tell it on your site. The aspiration is that as the category matures, an online search for your category name alone would reveal a number of high performing content assets that are hosted on your web properties.

However, online isn't the only channel for creating and distributing early stage content. In fact, live events and experiences are arguably even more powerful delivery vehicles for companies in new markets. We'll spend time in Chapter Eight talking about how to build and grow community and live events programs rooted in industry best practices. Whether online or experiential, the quality of your content is extremely important in new categories, as is the cadence of content delivery. Since there won't be incumbent channels for relevant industry best practices, keeping a steady drumbeat of blog releases, newsletters, webinars, events, etc. will keep the young market "tuned in" to your programming and engaged with what you have to say.

With so many potential topics to cover, how can you prioritize your content roadmap and know exactly what to write? I've found that there are three places to look in order to source content ideas:

1. **What are your customers telling you?** The best source of content ideas are from the market—What are your customers struggling with and where could they use support? Is it hiring the right person? Put together a sample job description and write a blog post about how to hire in your category. Is it the right meeting format to review progress? Host a webinar showcasing different agendas and approaches from companies that have figured it out.

2. **Where do you want to lead the market?** Ultimately you'll need conviction on where the market is headed, both informed by what your customers are telling you and by the true north vision that you're building for on your product roadmap. Seed out the story through best practices and education before you release new products and features into a community who doesn't understand them.

3. **What does the data reveal?** Eventually you'll want to make sure your content is performing well, meaning that it's driving the right type of engagement online and impacting business results. Sometimes the content that performs the best is not what your customers are asking for, nor anything particularly

novel, but rather a replay of the foundational questions that people regularly search for. Doubling down on the narratives of top performing assets with fresh ideas and approaches should drive good engagement.

5. Evangelize the Category as the Leaders of the Movement

As your content efforts start to bear fruit, eventually your brand will become recognized as the official torch-bearer and leader behind the movement of your category. Your company will be asked to speak at conferences, investor events, and local meetups. You'll be invited by customers to present at their all-hands meetings and company kick-offs. Although prioritizing executive time will only get more complex, opportunities to carry the torch for your industry are always well worth the effort in the long run.

One of the best evangelism investments that we made at Gainsight was agreeing to write the book on Customer Success, which was published by Wiley in 2016. Writing a book was by no means a small effort, but three years and 40,000+ copies sold later, we've developed a degree of credibility in having been both champions and evangelists of Customer Success since the early days of the profession. While some may wonder if people even read business books anymore, the reality is that writing the definitive book on our category has carried our brand to places we never thought we'd access with our online content efforts alone, including board rooms and investor meetings.

As I mentioned earlier in this chapter, I learned a lot about building content marketing programs from Marketo and some of the great evangelistic content they created in their "definitive guide" e-book series. One of the authors of a foundational piece of content that I learned a lot from was Maria Pergolino, an early marketing leader at the company who went on to serve in an SVP Marketing and CMO capacity at Apttus and Anaplan, respectively. Today, Maria is a celebrity in B2B marketing circles, having developed and shared her own playbook for building world-class go-to-market teams that drive growth, differentiation, and category leadership. I asked her to share her perspective on the intersection of content marketing and category creation, and what aspiring marketers should keep in mind when building and scaling their content marketing programs.

Ten Tips for Supercharging Your Content Marketing Program

By Maria Pergolino, Chief Marketing Officer (Previously at Anaplan, Apttus, Marketo)

Content marketing is changing almost as fast as technology itself. And because of this you may not be seeing the results you'd be expecting from your category creating content strategy. Let's grab a glass of wine and talk about why.

We all know that the buyer now controls the buying cycle. But why is this happening? And how can we make this work for us? Essentially, the Internet has brought an inconsumable amount of data to our fingertips, but decision making is more complex than ever, with bigger groups of people wanting a say in what is being purchased for a company. In fact, CEB, a Gartner company, suggests there are more people involved in making B2B buying decisions, growing from an average of 5.4 stakeholders in 2015 to 6.8 in 2017. Everyone gets a vote, but most aren't experts in what is being purchased, and many may not know a solution to solve the challenge even exists, especially when it's a new category like yours. I can't tell you how many times I've been talking to another executive who tells me how they solved a problem using a home-grown tool they or a consultant created taking up big budget and development resources to overcome a challenge when there is an out-of-the-box solution available at a lower cost.

(continued)

Ten Tips for Supercharging Your Content Marketing Program (*Cont'd*)

So how do we get buyers to purchase your category defining product, so this is avoided? The buyer has two options: ask the people in their network what to do (friends, influencers, or consultants) or go to the Internet, a conference, or maybe even buy a book (like this one!) to find a solution on their own. You need to be top of mind in the first approach, and your content must be front and center with the latter. Ensuring your brand comes up as the answer for that large buying team in both cases takes some effort, which is why we started with some wine. I'd also suggest reading in Chapter Nine about how to activate your customers as advocates and using these 10 content marketing tips:

1. **Is there a doctor in the house?** Ensure that buyers find your content when they search for answers to their problems. For example, when Marketo (and Eloqua and Pardot) were creating the Marketing Automation category, we were sharing tips on how to do marketing a better way, not about what the solution could do. This gave us an audience with our target buyer and allowed us to build credibility with them because we were helping ease their business pains.

2. **Face it, books are judged by the cover.** Ensure your content stands out from the overabundance of marketing materials currently available. If your content marketing strategy can be summarized with a list of blog posts and white papers, I can almost promise that you'll see limited success. So why are so many brands taking this approach? When content marketing was new, this worked, because there wasn't as much content available. But now our buyers

are in information overload, with attention spans getting shorter every day. This doesn't mean abandon your content strategy, but instead make sure it is highly compelling to your prospective buyer. An example you may have seen that does a great job creating compelling content is the blending of an iPhone, hockey puck, Rubik's Cube, and more via the Will It Blend series (willitblend.com) by Blendtec Total Blender. Instead of creating a white paper about how strong their blender is, they literally put their blender to the test, blending everyday items to educate their buyers. This marketing was so compelling it was featured in a Seth Godin book and made an appearance in a Weezer video.

3. **Cats (and content) have nine lives.** When companies start thinking about marketing a product, they often start by creating a website. The problem is, as we discussed, people don't know you, and your new category, exist, so they are not likely to show up on your homepage. Instead, you need to take all the different types of content you create and share it through various channels. This includes digital channels like LinkedIn, Facebook, Twitter, as well as industry websites, association websites, press releases, online communities, and more. This also includes physical locations to share content like sponsored trade shows, user groups, and hosted marketing events.

4. **Opportunity can't knock if it can't find the door.** Regardless of the type of content you create, you must make sure it gets found. Do this by optimizing the content for the channel where it is being featured. Every channel, whether it's in social media, something printed, or even email, has a different way to ensure it shows up

(continued)

**Ten Tips for Supercharging Your Content
Marketing Program (*Cont'd*)**

for your prospects. Figuring out how to optimize for each channel can take time, but there are many consultants and companies that help with this, from social media agencies to search engine optimization firms and more.

5. **All roads must lead to Rome (and your category).** I wholeheartedly agree with Anthony that we must leverage early-stage content in our category creation, but we also must let our buyer know what steps to take next. When we create content about a pain a customer is having, we can't just recognize their pain, but we must share how we can solve that pain, including how our customers have seen success and what they can do to see similar success.

6. **It's not rocket science, it's data science.** Many companies recognize how important it is to create great content and share it through different channels, but it's also important to make sure we know who that content is going to by having clean and up-to-date data about our prospects. For example, we can give Facebook a list of our desired customers and pay for ads to show up only to these people. Or we can do this by using channels like email or direct mail, where we send our content directly to our target purchaser. This drastically reduces the waste in our advertising, because we know who the content is going to. But it's only as good as the prospect data that we have, so it must be up-to-date and accurate.

7. **Waiter, content for one, please.** Content is often created for the masses, with one paper or video created to address the entire market. But if your product is a considered purchase, with few buyers who spend a lot on your

solution, you may find creating content for a single buyer or small group of buyers is a better strategy. This account-based content strategy is very company-to-human centric and can help prospects know how truly committed your company is to solve their pain, building trust.

8. **There's no I in Category.** No one voice creates a category alone. Check out the TedTalk named "How to Start a Movement" by Derek Sivers. In this talk he has the crowd laughing out loud because of a ridiculous dancer at a music festival. You can't help but think this dancing person is a bit crazy as he thrashes his arms in the air in the middle of a field. It's not until others join him that you think it might be fun, and thus, a huge groundswell is created. Earlier I mentioned how Marketo had competitors, like Eloqua and Pardot, that also created great content. We gave each other credibility by agreeing there was a problem and showed similar ways to solve the pains the marketer was facing. All the customer had to do was choose which solution to buy. In content marketing for category creation, competition is not the enemy. A second, more current example is from the emerging account-based marketing (ABM) category. This is an emerging category where content marketing has been abundant. An early entrant to the market was Demandbase, who was sharing content about account-based marketing for years with little growth. It wasn't until a strong competitor, Engagio, emerged that the category gained momentum, as this lent credibility to the entire space, with both brands benefitting.

9. **Hello, Madame President!** While there must be a competitor for there to be a category, you need to be the biggest, boldest, most credible and differentiated voice across

(continued)

Ten Tips for Supercharging Your Content Marketing Program (*Cont'd*)

the competition to become the leader in the category you are creating. You didn't come here to become vice president in your category, right? Being the first mover into the market does not make the leader (as Anthony highlighted in Chapter Three), but being the one with the momentum from great content does.

10. **The robots are taking over!** Finally, keep in mind that content creation is evolving. And while we still don't have robots fetching our slippers, machine learning now recommends content; AI, like Siri and Cortana, finds content for you; and IOT is bringing us content in new ways and places every day. Make sure your content is evolving as your customers do to ensure you stay in the front of your category.

7 | Create a Lifestyle Brand for Your Category

I have to confess something. While I've spent my entire career working in B2B, I am completely and hopelessly fascinated by B2C marketing. It's hard not to be as a marketer when you experience campaigns such as Airbnb's "Belong Anywhere" or basically anything that the teams at Disney, Nike, or Virgin America (a brand gone too soon) have produced.

B2C marketers are responsible for building and maintaining brands that speak to our very humanity as consumers, on a level that's so much deeper than just products and features. They are emotive—developing relationship with their audiences and influencing affinity and purchasing decisions at an almost subconscious level. I aspire to buy a Tesla not because I think the vehicles themselves are any more luxurious than their German or Italian peers, but rather, I want to experience the future of transportation and do my part to help accelerate the world's transition to sustainable energy. Prior to having children, my wife and I would make an annual pilgrimage to Disneyland, not because we were particularly passionate about theme parks, but because we wanted to access the wonder and imagination of our childhood. The B2C world understands the power of brand in driving business results, a notion from which those of us in B2B marketing can draw inspiration, but seldom activate in our day-to-day jobs of building and optimizing marketing funnels.

But the world is changing. The B2H reality that I described in Chapter Two suggests that the B2B and B2C worlds are collapsing together under the weight of consumer expectations both at home and at work. Today's marketer is challenged with solving for both short-term impact (feeding sales with enough leads to hit their number this quarter) and long-term impact of building a generational brand to last. In category creation specifically, striking a balance of both short- and long-term investments is critical. Participants in early markets will look to the market leader for both practical support on the day-to-day tactics within the category as well as long-term vision on where it's headed. In order to empower both, the best device at a marketer's disposal is still content marketing.

However, how many webinars have you watched in your personal life as a consumer? How many e-books (not from Amazon or Apple Books) have you downloaded for any reason other than work? As we discussed in Chapter Six, these form factors do indeed have an important place in your content marketing strategy, but are certainly table stakes for how businesses can deliver content to a professional audience. The future of B2H marketing will challenge *every* company to consider the same form factors and channels that end consumers interact with in their personal lives as opportunities to deliver value from the professional context. One of the underlying trends driving this imperative is the unbelievable success of one of the greatest categories created in the last two decades—Marketing Automation.

As more and more businesses developed content marketing programs and embraced the power of email as a distribution channel, our inboxes suddenly became *flooded* with content. Take a look at your email right now—some of the content sent to you by vendors is valuable, but for the most part, my assumption is that you'll find a lot of noise that somehow managed to slip through your spam filters. It's no surprise that the Marketing Automation category itself is evolving and being redefined to appreciate *experiences* for consumers on the other end of campaigns. Another response to the "noise problem" in email was the birth of the account-based marketing (ABM) category—a new approach to marketing that exhorts hyper-personalization of content and context delivered to a specific account (or hyper-targeted set of accounts), leveraging other channels outside of email such as display networks, direct mail, and the corporate website itself. The operating principle of ABM is that personalized campaigns will be much more effective than the alternative, eliminating any wasted effort and resources.

While ABM is a step in the right direction for Marketing Automation as a whole, it alone will not solve for the long-term brand-building motion that is required to create a category with widespread awareness successfully. In order to optimize for the long term, best of breed companies operating with a B2H mentality need to complement traditional content marketing (as discussed in the last chapter) with premium content and media programs that engage the consumers behind the logos they market and sell to. Like the traditional programs, premium content is not disconnected from growth and will undoubtedly have its place in the funnel—whether driving widespread awareness above it all or as a means of improving lead scores and uncovering buying intent within your market. The difference is the context from which the program is developed and inspired, where again, we look to our friends in B2C marketing who have already coined a term for this human approach to building affinity in the marketplace: lifestyle branding.

What Is a Lifestyle Brand?

You've likely never heard the words "lifestyle brand" uttered at a B2B company, but in the B2C world, the term is well understood. According to *Lifestyle Brands: A Guide to Aspirational Marketing* by Stefania Saviolo and Antonio Marazza, a lifestyle brand is "a company that markets its products or services to embody the interests, attitudes, and opinions of a group or a culture. Lifestyle brands seek to inspire, guide, and motivate people, with the goal of their products contributing to the definition of the consumer's way of life." Several examples of lifestyle brands come to mind—companies like Nike that have shaped culture around sports and fitness, or Harley-Davidson who developed attitudinal loyalty within their passionate fan base around the common ideal of freedom. These brands deliver so much more than just athletic equipment and motorcycles, but authentic and emotional stories of representative people in their audience who see life through a different lens. Those stories bind their audience together in the spirit of that shared perspective, creating affinity for the brand and, ultimately, selling more athletic equipment and motorcycles.

One of the best examples of lifestyle branding is Red Bull, the creators of the energy drink category. That's the product they sell, but what they market is adrenaline, performance, and living life to the extreme. While Gatorade and other sports drinks were dominating the brand index of mainstream athletics, Red Bull saw an opportunity to go where their competitors were not investing and build affinity with a somewhat marginalized industry of sports that include surfing, climbing, skydiving, cliff diving, skateboarding, and others. The alignment to their brand promise was obvious, like some of the beverages they compete with, traditional sports were not quite extreme enough for the Red Bull consumer. They began to colonize these *other* sports categories as *extreme* sports, a community of athletes and individuals who were bound together by their shared passions for adrenaline.

Today, a simple glance at their website will reveal where Red Bull is focusing their marketing: a dedicated media studio that creates content for their audience, engages influencers within the community, and produces stunts that literally put athletes at the edge of the earth's atmosphere. At the heart of it all—content. Content that champions the identity of their subculture, shines a light on their activities, and fosters interaction between members of the community. Building a lifestyle brand for extreme living has paid off for Red Bull, who according to Caffeine Informer, continues to dominate as the energy drink category globally and has captured 43% of the total energy drink sales in the United States in 2018.[1]

---

[1] James Foster, "Top Selling Energy Drink Brands," Caffeine Insider, February 7, 2019, https://www.caffeineinformer.com/the-15-top-energy drink-brands

Developing premium content to create culture around your category will impact your bottom line and, beyond that, will cultivate and engage a faithful community around your brand that can last for generations.

Thinking about your content marketing philosophy as a lifestyle brand for the community in your new category is a powerful way to optimize for both short- and long-term outcomes. While articulating the "why" and educating on the "how" of your category are important, the way that the content is produced and delivered can help create and contribute to the culture of your community. For companies creating categories within the business context, an analog for lifestyle brand would be career companion—the sum of your content marketing efforts can inspire, guide, and motivate the professional development of the people in your community. Can your brand aspire to "do life" with those in the role that you serve? The answer is yes—by investing in the development of premium content and unlocking channels that are still relatively untapped from traditional B2B companies.

Digital Media

With the cost to produce high quality video content dramatically dropping (4K 1080p resolution now standard on all new iPhones) and social media continuing to connect our personal and professional lives, the opportunity to create and distribute high quality video content has never been easier. Going a step or two beyond the iPhone, many companies are building in-house video production studios with basic lighting kits, SLR cameras, and microphones for less than $10,000. According to Vidyard's 2019 State of Video in Business Report, "a whopping 82% of businesses reported greater investments in video in 2018 and Vidyard's B2B clients published 83% more videos on a monthly basis compared to the previous year."[2] While video

---

[2] "2019 State of Video in Business Report," Vidyard, 2019, https://www.vidyard.com/state-of-video-report/

continues to be popular for middle and late stage content assets such as recorded demos and customer testimonials, the idea of developing episodic, early stage content around the "why" and "how" of your category is where the innovation is headed.

Video will also add a face to your category, which can benefit both external and internal spokespeople. Featuring customers or non-customer members of the community is a great way to appeal to the novelty and status motivators of the early adopters in your category and provide them an opportunity to share their stories. Since video is an extremely engaging medium, the likelihood of creating a network effect around that content when shared in their networks will benefit both of your brands. Internally, video is an incredible mechanism to live your values and culture out loud and to build authenticity and trust in the market by positioning your executives as the embodiment of those virtues. In Chapter Eleven, we will take a closer look at how leveraging video in your executive communications strategy can become a superpower for your category leadership effort.

An emerging aspect of digital media is the introduction of *live* video—a channel that allows your audience to experience your brand and content efforts in a more raw and unrehearsed format. Live video streaming capability is now standard on most social networks (including LinkedIn) and can be created using anything from an iPhone to an SLR camera with professional encoder. At Gainsight, we were inspired to experiment with live video streaming during the 2014 FIFA World Cup. We noticed that every office we would visit during work hours, including our own, would have a soccer game streaming live on monitors prominently located in common spaces. We asked ourselves if we could create content for our community that's *so engaging* that people would literally take time away from work to watch it together as a team.

That's where the idea for PulseCheck was born—an all day live workshop that goes deep on the top seven sessions from our Pulse conference earlier in the year. The general principle was that conferences are great (more on that in the next chapter), but given the breadth of content on the agenda, they are difficult programs to go extremely deep into any one topic. PulseCheck became an all day live experience that did just that—and every year will drive 1 to 1.5x the number of registrations than we do to our live conference. We also wanted to build a culture around PulseCheck, which like the World Cup, would spawn viewing parties at customer sites within our community. We promoted a viewing party campaign that challenged our audience to cancel all non-critical calls for the day, reserve a conference room, and commit to broadcasting PulseCheck all day as a free team-building exercise. For teams that drove the most registrations, or were on our named account list, we would cater meals to their offices in order to supplement their viewing experience. Although this may sound a bit like an all-day webinar (which technically it was), live video changed that perception in the minds of our audience and turned the would-be webinar into a live global experience for the Customer Success industry.

It's worth considering other forms of digital media outside of video. I hinted at this earlier in the book, but a somewhat crazy campaign that we ran at Gainsight was to record and distribute a hip-hop song for our category called *Customer Success (Who's Fired Up?)* on Spotify, Apple Music, and everywhere else music is available. Yes, you read that right. We hired a performer, booked studio time at Capitol Records in Los Angeles, and produced a song that we positioned as the official anthem for our community. The idea behind the campaign was that our audience was on Spotify and Apple Music in their consumer lives anyway, and yet if they happened to search for Customer Success or Gainsight on those platforms, they would find nothing. What if instead on their way into the office one morning, they could discover a song that would get them fired up for work that day? What if in a very small (and maybe even random) way, we can serve them in the unlikeliest of places for an enterprise software company? The campaign ended up being wildly successful, but we didn't truly know how successful it was until our customers would film music videos lip syncing to the song and send them to us—a crazy example of a point I made in Chapter Five, that communities can reflect the culture of the category leader.

Beyond recording hip-hop singles, there's one other form factor for digital media that has become increasingly popular in both B2B and B2C playbooks. Have you listened to a podcast lately? The data suggests that you probably have—over 51% of the U.S. population has listened to one of the 660,000+ podcasts currently available online.[3] In fact, podcast listeners have consumed an average of seven different shows per week in 2018, up from five in 2017. Like their digital media counterpart in videos, podcasts are great (and cost-effective) ways to create rich early stage content about industry best practices and feature the voices and insights of the community. According to Edison Research's *Infinite Dial 2019* report, 49% of podcast listening is done at home and 22% while driving in a vehicle,[4] unlocking new opportunities for your audience to catch up on your content while not at the office. The cost to produce podcasts are relatively low as well—ranging from a laptop and software subscription, to developing an in-house studio for a few thousand dollars, to leveraging a specialized third-party agency such as Sweet Fish Media to run your podcast operations on your behalf. Whatever your approach, create the official podcast for your category before any of your competitors beat you to the punch.

Education and Career Services

People consume information in different ways—in fact, there are seven distinct learning styles that humans can employ. We often prefer a mix of several different styles, but one is dominant in the following categories:

1. *Visual (spatial):* Prefer using pictures, images, and spatial understanding.
2. *Aural (auditory-musical):* Prefer using sound and music.

---

[3] Ross Winn, "2019 Podcast Stats & Facts (New Research from Mar 2019)," Podcast Insights, March 6, 2019, https://www.podcastinsights.com/podcast-statistics/
[4] "The Infinite Dial 2019," Edison Research and Triton Digital, March 6, 2019, https://www.edisonresearch.com/infinite-dial-2019/

3. *Verbal (linguistic):* Prefer using words, both in speech and writing.
4. *Physical (kinesthetic):* Prefer using your body, hands, and sense of touch.
5. *Logical (mathematical):* Prefer using logic, reasoning, and systems.
6. *Social (interpersonal):* Prefer to learn in groups or with other people.
7. *Solitary (intrapersonal):* Prefer to work alone and use self-study.

With education being such an important aspect of content marketing programs for early categories, marketers have a responsibility to create content that appeals to each of the seven learning styles above. One of the best methods for doing this is to work with an instructional designer to create an industry certification course (or catalogue of courses) that articulates the fundamentals and skills required for success in the new category. While this may sound complicated to execute, the "how to" content you've committed to creating in Chapter Six is where most of the heavy lifting is. An instructional designer can take the content you've already created, curate it into learning pathways, and deliver an educational experience for your audience through the lens of a learning management system (LMS).

The benefits of creating an industry certification program are many, especially since consumers will apply a premium to learn from the market leader. These programs are typically promoted at the top-of-funnel, meaning anyone can sign up for the online, self-paced courses without necessarily being a customer. You may decide to charge for the courses and generate revenue (perhaps to offset a portion of that over-stretched marketing budget). You could give the courses away, or at least a subset away for free, in order to seed the market. However you choose to price the offering, an industry certification program is a great way to drive online conversions and engagement from members or perspective members of your community. Additionally, these programs can be leveraged by Sales during a contract negotiation in order to sweeten the deal terms and protect any revenue on the product sale. Partners love industry certification too—especially if they have an opportunity to co-develop some of the coursework or co-brand the offering and sell licenses into their audiences as well. Eventually, you'll know you're successful when the program is growing your database, helping Sales close deals, and program graduates are displaying their certifications proudly on their LinkedIn profiles and résumés.

In the B2B context, a formal education program will often go hand-in-hand with career services. As category leaders, the market will make an assumption that your company is the go-to authority for not just *how* to be successful in the category discipline, but *who* is doing it really well. This will inevitably lead to a number of inquiries from the market for introductions to capable executives and practitioners in your network for open positions. Informally, keeping a spreadsheet record of candidates who may be passively looking for new opportunities may be a helpful exercise to aid in conversations like these. Besides, what better way to build a relationship with a potential client than by helping their leader (and your future executive sponsor) land an exciting new opportunity? You might also consider building a more formal program around career services for both hiring managers and active job seekers in your category.

An easy way to build a formal career services program is to launch an online job board for members of your community to post and apply to open job requisitions. If you've successfully transformed your corporate website into the online home for your category, the traffic on your site is extremely targeted and of high value to both job seekers and hiring managers. Give those visitors an opportunity to interact directly with the job board-of-record for your category in order to find new career opportunities, and consider pulling in curated data feeds from other online sources to keep the listings active and up-to-date. The best news of all—building a job board is very cheap and easy as WordPress themes are available on ThemeForest .net for $49 and can power the entire program. All you need to do is brand the experience and integrate the new job board into your corporate website. By developing value-added education and career service programs into the lifestyle brand for your category, you are sending a signal to the market that you care deeply and thoughtfully about their success and will walk with them along their journey. In Chapter Twelve, I'll give you the tools you need to talk to your CFO about how these programs will also drive revenue—a powerful and important side-effect of driving success for your customers in new markets.

One of the companies in the marketplace that has done a phenomenal job of building a lifestyle brand around their category is Drift, the leading Conversational Marketing platform that turns website traffic into qualified meetings. Drift's VP of marketing David Gerhardt (affectionately known as "DG") is helping pioneer this new era of business-to-human marketing, and in building the Conversational Marketing category, is writing his own playbook on how to leverage digital media and creative activations to build a community around the concept of bringing humanity back into marketing. I asked DG what he has learned on his journey in building a lifestyle brand for marketers, and how that strategy has created a halo effect around the Drift brand. Here are five of the principles that he shared:

1. **Become a Student of the Game.** From his early days at the company, DG was encouraged to read business books to help shape his thinking on how to build the marketing team at Drift. However, in addition to classic B2B books such as *Behind the Cloud* and *Innovator's Dilemma*, he took to some brand marketing classics like *Ogilvy on Advertising* and *The 22 Immutable Laws of Branding*. Following his curiosity, he studied iconic consumer/CPG branding case studies like Procter & Gamble and Unilever to uncover how marketers outside of B2B differentiate in the marketplace by focusing on brand. There's something profound behind DG's curiosity here for B2B marketers—that inspiration for building a B2H marketing strategy may not come from peers in the industry, but from the lessons we can adapt from consumer and brand-oriented companies. Applying this learning at Drift, DG has become an early pioneer of B2H marketing and has built the foundations

of an incredible brand with a loyal following and aspirations of category dominance.

2. **Understand the Signal-to-Noise Ratio in Content Channels.** Signal-to-noise ratio is a science and engineering concept that compares the levels of a desired signal to the level of background noise. A ratio higher than 1:1 (greater than 0 decibels) indicates more signal than noise. As we discussed earlier in the chapter, the signal-to-noise ratio in content marketing today is off the charts. Increasingly, every company has a blog, webinar program, and maybe even a podcast. Even if your company has the highest quality of information that's completely relevant to your target audience, the channel capacity within email and our social feeds will almost certainly limit your ability to get that content in the right hands. So how do you stand out? DG recommends trying new channels when they're early and relatively green field from a noise perspective. Imagine the effectiveness of online marketing campaigns when companies first rolled out corporate email accounts—hello 85% open rates! One of the channels that DG leveraged early was LinkedIn video, a powerful and engaging method to connect and build a relationship with your professional network. With only his iPhone in hand and something profound to share, DG was able to break through the noise of the LinkedIn newsfeed and contribute to the marketing discussion in an authentic way.

3. **Zig While the Competition Zags.** DG knew that the way Drift was going to win in the market was not to out-Adwords the best "Adwordser" in the market, but rather, to find a way to stand out by breaking through the noise and focusing on brand. It's a simple idea at the surface, but profound in the context of category creation—how can we go where our competitors are not? The key to zigging, DG believes, is deep empathy for the customer. What could the Drift team create if *they themselves* were on the other end of the campaign? That thinking gave way to the Drift Insider program, a free content

subscription from Drift that includes exclusive interviews with authors, management lessons from the brightest minds in business, how-to sessions at the whiteboard from top leaders in sales, marketing, and product, expert-level Conversational Marketing and sales education, and other themes of premium content programs. That's the type of content that DG and the Drift team would choose to engage with to unlock growth in their own business and careers—not yet another vendor webinar. Nobody wants to be sold to—and as DG says, we as an industry have actually become *allergic* to sales in our consumer lives. Coming up with content programs that zig into the white space in the market while others zag can create meaningful engagement within our community, and pass that ever-important BS meter that has hardened our hearts as consumers.

4. **People Are Willing to Pay for Premium Content.** With the success of the Inbound Marketing and Marketing Automation categories, content has become somewhat of a commodity. Almost the entire library of the world's information is only one Google search or "Hey, Siri" away. It wasn't always this way. We can all remember a time when information was much more scarce—where ESPN dominated the sports conversation while CNN *was* our source of global news. Today there are thousands of sources of information, and understanding which sources are trusted over others has increasingly become a challenge. This has led to a new reality where customers are willing to pay for content that they can trust and deem better than what's readily available for free. The old adage of "you get what you pay for" may be true in this context—consumer buying patterns have signaled a willingness to pay for content that's perceived as exclusive or comes at a high quality of production. Consider recent consumer examples such as Apple News+, Disney+, or ESPN+ that are paid premium offerings on top of the core services that are typically available for free or cheap. DG believes that charging for content is a great conversation starter, and

with the success of the Drift Insider+ program, the data supports his vision for this. Charging for professional development content can be a great way to access budget within your target market outside of software, and perhaps with the blessing of your CFO, even self-fund the creation and distribution of the marketing program itself.

5. **The Publishing Industry Still Matters.** I noticed that Drift had published several books, and after talking to DG about this, I wondered if there was any correlation behind these programs and his passion for reading. As it turns out, one of the company's core values is Students & Teachers, which inspires a culture of always learning from and teaching one another. The reality is that anyone can write a 300-word blog post—we see examples in our everyday lives of armchair quarterbacks weighing in on "best practices" online in 280 characters or less. Writing a book, on the other hand, is a statement—or in DG's words, a book is *a book*. It takes a lot of effort to really pour your heart into 60,000+ words and make it real, signaling to the world the depth of thought and intention that went into putting that piece of content together. The reports of the death of publishing, as it were, are greatly exaggerated. DG suggests that not only is self-publishing easier than ever, but printing books (rather than distributing them online) is not an expensive exercise. The market will place a premium on physical copies over digital given the rationale above, and making physical copies available to the community is a great way to delight. If you're creating a category, writing *the* book on your category is a competitive brand advantage all to itself.

By focusing on bringing the humanity back to marketing, DG and the Drift team are helping usher in this brand new era of B2H marketing. The net effect of these programs and others have solidified Drift's leadership position in Conversational Marketing—the category that they themselves are creating. Another outcome of their efforts has been the development and curation of a passionate and loyal community of brand advocates (whether customers or otherwise) who look to Drift for leadership on how to drive marketing outcomes and self-actualize in their careers along the way. Community is one of the most impactful content delivery vehicles for category creators, and when done right, can build a competitive moat around your brand unlike any other program.

8 | Grow a Community by Doubling Down on Live Events and Experiences

What is it about in-person experiences that gives us energy as humans? In our personal lives, we spend money to go to concerts and sing along to the same songs we hear on the radio, or attend sporting events to root for the same team that we can watch on TV. We pay a premium for these experiences—perhaps to be in the same venue as the stars that we idolize, or to post a selfie that proves to our social circles that we were actually there (admit it, you know it's true). Maybe instead it's more about community—an innate desire within all of us to share in experiences with other fans bonded and brought together by a common cause. These are *strangers* we've never met before, but when together, we are united by the lyrics to the songs we know by heart and the stat lines of our favorite players. When we feel the weight of being hyper-connected digitally—yet so alone in a broken world—community gives us the sense of belonging that we so desperately desire.

The pursuit of connection and belonging is hardcoded into our psychology as humans and is not a toggle that can be intentionally switched on/off when at work. This is one of the core principles of business-to-human marketing that's so often underappreciated— the imperative to craft messaging and create programs that can serve employees, customers, and the market at large in their quest for belonging within their teams, companies, and industries. Within the context of category creation specifically, facilitating the development and growth of community around your market is vital to success. The unmet need you've identified in the market is the common cause that binds your audience together, similar to the concert and sporting event examples that I referenced earlier. Unlike those examples, however, which have established fan bases to begin with, the early chapters of a new category can often feel very lonely for those who are participating. There can be an overwhelming feeling of being alone in figuring out how to solve that problem, realizing that there are not enough resources to be effective, or navigating a lack of empowerment to contribute to strategy.

That's where community marketing comes in—a purposeful and authentic effort to gather the early adopters of your category and advance their interests through a variety of programs. There is nothing more powerful in category creation than having those same individuals who are carrying the weight of the market problem be taken in and accepted by their tribe, feeling that perhaps for the first time in a long time they are not alone. In a world where products are increasingly on a glide path toward commoditization, a brand's community enforces a competitive moat around the business and creates significant enterprise value. Salesforce refers to their community as *Trailblazers*, while Marketo calls their faithful the *Marketing Nation*. In both examples, community isn't limited to paying customers of their products, but anyone within their audience who cares about the category. At Gainsight, we tend to think about our marketable database as the measuring stick of what our community looks like and how it's growing.

Early in the company's history, we had observed that Customer Success managers would meet in office parks around Silicon Valley to connect and learn from each other. We made an early bet (between our Seed and Series A rounds of funding) to organize an industry conference that would gather as many folks from the community together as would come, all in the spirit of sharing Customer Success best practices and networking. The conference, called Pulse, drew over 300 attendees and would become the proof point from which we would base our entire marketing strategy. The best part of our first conference, however, could not be measured—it was the palpable energy and spirit of the community that felt impossible to manufacture. This pervasive feeling of belonging that, *"Finally, I'm around other people who are just like me."*

Another compelling attribute about community is that, by its very nature, it compounds as your lifestyle brand develops around the category. Members who find value in your content and programming tell their colleagues, who enroll into your thought leadership by filling out a web form. In the seven years since our inaugural Pulse conference in 2013, the conference has grown by 20x and has spawned sister events in the United Kingdom and Australia. A huge part of that growth has been driven by how the brand has developed organically, which shows up in the massive expansion of our marketable database. Building a content marketing program (as we discussed in Chapters Six and Seven) is a critical component of growing and engaging the community to help create the compounding flywheel—however, digital programs can never be a replacement for the live experience.

Creating Experiences, Not Events

Live events have become a critical part of the marketing stack in recent years. As part of their Event Marketing 2019 Benchmark and Trends report, event technology company Bizzabo found that most (41%) marketers believe that events are the single-most effective marketing channel over digital advertising, email marketing, and content marketing, reflecting a 32% increase since 2017.[1] Beyond that, the number of companies organizing 20 or more events per year increased by 17% between 2017 and 2018. As the volume of events in the marketplace continues to grow, there's never been a more critical time to build event programs that stand out from the noise. This challenge has led to the popularization of a new trend in event marketing circles around creating *experiences* rather than events, a strategy that places a

---

[1] Anna Sang, "2019 Event Marketing Statistics, Trends and Data," The Bizzabo Blog, December 17, 2018, https://blog.bizzabo.com/event-marketing-statistics

creative premium on activating an emotive and sensory journey for attendees that cultivates human connection and relationship.

We've all been to corporate events that are not experiences—maybe the all day seminar hosted at the Airport Radisson in the room without windows, and eating the barely passable lunch options while counting the minutes until happy hour. The content and learning may have been important, but you'll dread attending the next one. Meanwhile, in our consumer lives, we've attended music festivals such as the Coachella Valley Music and Arts Festival that create incredible experiences that enhance the musical performances, or urban pop-ups such as the Museum of Ice Cream that are designed intentionally to trigger emotive and sensory experiences. Those examples are the new bar and what we are competing against even in the corporate context—a new approach that requires a whole new set of considerations for event marketers.

The details matter when creating corporate experiences—focusing on the little things that often are overlooked when planning corporate events such as the music that's played as attendees enter the room, the quality of the food being served, or how to manage energy throughout the day. The details play a major role in how attendees network with others and retain the information they learn at your event. In many ways, event experiences become another "product" for your business and should be managed that way. Experiences also put your company culture on display for your community to witness firsthand, which as I described in Chapter Five, is a powerful way to build brand equity with the market as category leaders.

Types of Corporate Experiences

Four types of experiences are relevant and valuable in category creation, all of which play distinct roles in building and growing community: field events, community groups, executive forums, and industry conferences.

- **Field Events.** While traditionally considered sales-led efforts to generate and accelerate pipeline in new markets, field events are an invaluable way to push category thought leadership out beyond your corporate headquarters and into the community. These programs have been traditionally organized as dinners or private events, but many companies have also developed road show programs that get executives and customers out into the regions sharing best practices around the category. That's the key nuance for field events in the category creation context— leading with best practices over product demos and sales pitches. Sales will certainly be able to prospect for revenue opportunity, but bringing people together in their local markets to inspire, educate, and connect will create exponential value for the brand and put sales in a better position to prospect.

- **Community Groups.** Unlike field events, community groups are self-managed chapters of category aficionados organized by volunteer local leaders and run somewhat autonomously to your company. Think user groups, but not necessarily comprised only of customers. Given the compounding effect of community, these programs serve as great opportunities to create and grow a brand presence in major cities exhibiting category energy, even if you don't have a local team or office there. Think about it this way—you are building a marketable database in key cities across the globe anyway, supporting a local leader in promoting a meetup is only one (focused) email away. Community groups also impact market development efforts and can help the company make data-driven decisions on where to focus or build dedicated operations. The value for local leader leaders is there too, as they have an opportunity to build their professional brands and be affiliated with a category.

- **Executive Forums.** Since executives will not usually attend large scale conferences unless they're speaking or participating in meetings onsite, executive forums can package that same thought leadership energy into a more intimate format that's appropriate for a group of senior leaders. This audience will care more about the strength of the attendee list and which of their peers will be in attendance than anything else. Forums are typically invite-only, high-touch experiences that are a mix of facilitated small group practicums and large group readouts. The truth is that executives get far more value from learning from each other than from listening to a speaker deliver a keynote. In fact, Marketing spends more time organizing the attending executives into small groups (by company size, vertical and other vectors) than any other aspect of the planning effort. At Gainsight, we found that partnering with a professional facilitator/executive coach to help both develop the curriculum and guide the experience has been an extremely valuable way to ensure resonance for our executive attendees. In early markets where strategy definition often precedes a technology purchase—executive forums provide category creators an opportunity to engage decision makers and accelerate the path to a sales conversation.

- **Industry Conferences.** Over the last decade, corporate event teams have developed a new program at the heart of their strategy—industry conferences. Unlike user and partner conferences (which have been around for some time), companies of all sizes are moving the conference marketing strategy up-funnel and are hosting industry-oriented events as a means of, among other outcomes, establishing thought leadership in their new categories. When done right, industry conferences can become powerful displays of category leadership for the organizers— the growth in attendees signaling the momentum behind the category you're building. It's an opportunity for your executive team to set the tone for where the category is headed and to put teammates, customers, and prospects on stage to contribute to that conversation. From the attendee perspective, conferences have become a familiar part of the career journey. Business professionals regularly attend conferences seeking inspiration from industry luminaries, education and learning from best practices shared by those a few steps ahead, and authentic human connection with peers in the community.

While each of these experience types certainly has its merits, the program with the most seismic impact in category creation is developing an industry conference. Conferences check every box in our human pursuit of belonging—powerful activations that create a halo effect around category, community, and brand. It's no surprise that conferences have become increasingly popular for most companies, but absolutely critical for category creators. Early markets need an annual destination for education and connection, and being the brand that can deliver that value creates sustainable competitive advantage. But the idea of developing an industry conference from scratch sounds complicated and expensive. Where do you begin?

How to Plan an Industry Conference for Your Category

While planning an industry conference is primarily the responsibility of the Marketing team, make no mistake, it ends up being a company-wide effort. The annual event becomes a rallying call for each department across the business to drive toward, whether that's Engineering readying a new product or feature to release, Marketing launching new and refreshed messaging, or the Customer Success team preparing new services and education offerings. As a result, well-executed industry conferences can impact every aspect of the business in profound ways, including generating net new pipeline, accelerating existing pipeline, increasing product adoption, driving higher net retention, and fostering teammate engagement.

Creating an organizational culture around the planning effort for your conference is critical, but for the marketers given the charter, there are seven important principles to keep in mind.

1. Make It About the Movement, Not Your Product

One of the key distinctions of an *industry* conference over others is the complete focus on category best practices over company product and sales pitches. We have spent a lot of time going into detail in Chapter Six on why this is important from a content marketing point of view, but the separation of church and state is exponentially more sacred at industry conferences. Attendees invest time and budget to attend these programs in order to learn and network, and not to be forced into a surprise sales pitch. If you violate that trust, they will not be afraid to let you or the general public know on social media, the event mobile app, or the Net Promoter Score (NPS) survey afterward. In early markets while you're still building brand equity in the category, just having your company logo as the host of the event is enough. The market is smart enough to recognize and appreciate the company behind the program, and if they gain real value from attending, will give you due credit as the organizer and thought leader. If you're able to continue to walk that fine line and maintain that trust with your audience, you'll find that conference demographics will typically skew heavier toward prospects than customers. Seven years into planning Pulse conferences at Gainsight, more than 60% of our attendees come from prospect (non-customer) accounts, a reflection of the registration campaigns driven into our marketable database and the focus of our sales and SDR teams. Our intention is for all of our attendees—whether customers or otherwise—to feel inspired at the conference, that they've chosen the right profession, and that by being pioneers of the new category are playing their small part in advancing the community and movement forward.

Over time the line between industry best practices and product innovation can blur, especially as the category matures, customer attendees grow (on an absolute basis), and the notion of procuring products within the category becomes more understood. In fact, eventually, the pendulum can swing the other way entirely as some of your attendees will want to hear *more* about your product than perhaps you were initially willing to share. Knowing when to start turning up that dial is tricky, but you can experiment by announcing product-oriented tracks that are clearly identified breakouts on the agenda. Attendees shouldn't be surprised to find themselves in a product-oriented session, but instead, should seek it out intentionally. Once the category really matures and your product becomes synonymous with innovation in the category, experiment with a product keynote in front of the entire general session. We introduced a product innovation keynote at Pulse in our fifth year and did not hear any negative feedback from the audience. In fact, our learning from the qualitative comments in our survey were that they appreciated seeing what's coming next from a product perspective—whether they were customers or not.

2. Source Speakers Who Add Credibility and Validate the Category

One of the insecurities that comes with launching a conference brand from scratch is whether or not anyone will show up—a fear that, being new to the market, there isn't enough credibility in your brand to justify paid admission to the event. While there might be some rational thinking there, the best way to build and scale the credibility of your program (every year) is by leveraging the brand equity of your speakers. Having an impressive speaker roster serves many purposes, but principally, it signals to the world that a collection of the best minds in the industry, from reputable and notable companies, have something to say about your category. What better validation than that? Beyond driving registrations, having great speakers at the conference signals to those in attendance that they've chosen the right career path and are indeed critical to the success of the business.

While building an exciting speaker roster is important to the credibility and impact of your conference, so is understanding the different types of speakers and the distinct role they play within your agenda. Figure 8.1 illustrates the three types of speakers that each industry conference should include: VIP keynotes, executives, and practitioners. The design of the illustration is intentional, as companies should only consider paying for one or a few keynotes while

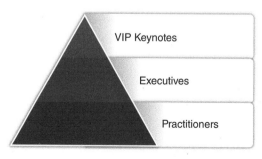

Figure 8.1 Three Types of Speakers at Industry Conferences

your target buyers and users can make up the long tail of your agenda. Let's walk through the details of each.

- **VIP Keynotes.** At the very top of the pyramid are keynotes, (typically) paid speakers who are either represented by a speaker bureau or otherwise require an honorarium to participate. These can be famous celebrities, athletes, authors, philanthropists, politicians, or other notable individuals who make themselves available to speak at events—often at a non-trivial cost. You'll also encounter "career speakers" who are on the circuit, effectively speaking at events all year round. Contracting one or a few of these speakers is typically a good idea for your conference, as their celebrity becomes a "draw" for prospective attendees, adding instant credibility to your event. Their participation is also a great thing for the attendees at the show, who look forward to hearing these individuals speak or maybe even getting an opportunity to sneak a selfie. For the most part both celebrities and career speakers will have little functional knowledge about your category—but that's ok. The purpose they serve isn't to be subject matter experts, but rather to contribute to the buzz and excitement about the conference brand you're building. The challenge is that this tier of speaker is typically pretty expensive, ranging anywhere from $5k–$500k per engagement, and well into the $1M+ range for the Oprahs of the world. If you do decide to anchor your conference around a paid keynote, take advantage of their presence at the conference by negotiating other activations around their stage time into the contract up-front— whether that's a meet and greet with VIPs or book signing.
- **Executives.** Once you've identified an anchor VIP keynote as a draw (whether you paid for him or her or not), the rest of your general session/keynote stage should be represented by chief executives from companies in your target demographic. Whether CEOs or some other senior leader from brands that your attendees would find both relevant and aspirational, these speakers will add credibility to your event and give the audience a lot of practical validation that what they're working on matters. This is especially important in early markets where the pursuit of belonging is often exacerbated by an insecurity as to whether or not senior leadership recognizes your efforts. These executive speakers will very rarely

charge an honorarium, but view their participation in conferences like yours as part of their executive communications strategy. With that being the case, getting executives to commit is no small effort, as they are extremely busy and selective with their time. At Gainsight we typically focus on sourcing executive speakers from our customer accounts first, but will also engage executives from target prospects/accounts as a way to develop a relationship with them. In the long-term greed of category creation, relationships matter, and giving executives a stage to share their perspectives as thought leaders in your new category is powerful.

- **Practitioners.** The majority of speakers at your conference ought to be target buyers, users, or administrators of your products and services. While keynotes and executive speakers can both inspire your audience and educate them at a very high level, attendees will typically want to go deep on topics that require the domain expertise that only practitioners carry. These speakers can typically be at the director/VP level for most organizations. Users/admins can lead practical sessions and workshops that benefit the individual contributors and front-line managers who attend the conference. Like executive speakers, there is rarely an expectation of paying for practitioner speakers; in fact it's quite the opposite. In time as your conference brand becomes recognized as the industry event of record for your category, a premium will be placed on the opportunity to speak there. These become career moments for members of your growing community—an opportunity to share their learning on the industry's biggest stage.

Ultimately, as the event hosts and stewards of the community, the responsibility lies within you to source speakers who come from reputable companies, have a great story to tell, and can deliver that story in a compelling way that connects with the audience. Checking all three boxes is difficult in planning, as sometimes the biggest names from the biggest companies in your network can draw a big crowd, but disappoint when they get on stage. You can likely find videos of prospective speakers on YouTube to get a better idea of their stage presence prior to extending an invitation to participate.

Doing Your Part—Diversity and Inclusion at Events
By: Lauren Sommers, VP Corporate Marketing at Gainsight

If you have not thought about a diversity and inclusion (D&I) strategy for events, choose to make this a priority right now. Diversity and inclusion is not a communications or HR strategy, but rather a critical path to creating cultured events and experiences where equal opportunity and representation are available to all. Events are by nature microcosms of community—anthropomorphic programs that give a human face to your industry as represented by the individuals both on stage and in the hallways. As event marketers, we need to work together to disrupt the current state of diversity and inclusion at corporate events in a meaningful way. We have a responsibility to be part of the change that shapes the future of event marketing by creating experiential platforms for anyone with a compelling story to tell, regardless of age, race, gender, sexual orientation, religious beliefs, socioeconomic status, education level, or any other underrepresented attributes. It's the right thing to do, but beyond that, diversity makes our events better and more representative of the wide array of voices in our community.

If you are thinking to yourself, "Where does one even begin to develop a D&I strategy for event programs?" you're not alone. The reality is that most companies are being challenged to think about this in a meaningful way for the very first time. As an industry, we started the dialogue around gender balance on the speaker agenda, but a world class D&I strategy at events goes well beyond gender. Here are some important things to think about when developing your event D&I program:

1. Make sure your company values are aligned with your event D&I strategy. Live experiences are powerful opportunities to live those values out loud.

2. Think about D&I across all aspects of your event, not just speakers. Cast a wider net for attendee recruitment, offer flexible registration options, and consider incorporating sessions on diversity itself.

3. Set goals that allow you to create a work back plan that holds you accountable to achieve them. Measure progress toward diversity goals throughout the planning process.

4. Fill your speaker pool with as many diverse speakers as possible—beyond just gender. There are several great resources online for identifying great conference speakers from diverse backgrounds.

5. Provide branding opportunities—think about how you can shine light on the diversity within your community in prominent ways.

6. Develop a meaningful D&I policy on your event website. Share your intention and open your doors for ideas and ways to include others.

7. Think about ways you can provide free or discounted tickets to underrepresented groups who can't gain access to your event. Many companies have developed a scholarship program to help offset attendance costs.

8. *Don't* use this as a PR opportunity. Your actions will speak louder than any words.

9. Own up to any mistakes. While there will always be room for improvement, taking an honest and self-aware position on the progress you're making is good for both your brand and other event marketers, who are all learning together.

By doing your part to create diverse event experiences that are inclusive and representative, you will only contribute to the leadership equity you've built in your category and growing community.

3. Build an Agenda That Inspires and Educates

While there are many aspects of the conference experience that stick with attendees long after the event is over, nothing is more critical to get right than the quality of the content represented in the agenda. Remember that the primary reason that people attend industry conferences is to learn—withholding any real learning from the sessions at your event can be catastrophic for both conference and category leadership. A good starting point on this effort is to map out all attendee personas (individual contributors, technical admins, people managers, and so on) and ensure that each of them has a curated journey and experience at the show, identifying any gaps that you might discover. Also consider the different form factors for session types—panels, fireside chats, keynotes, TED-style "flash" talks, workshops, or something different entirely. Panels, as an example, are becoming less popular with audiences unless restricted to only two or three panelists since the content is often not deep enough given time constraints. Regardless of session type, make sure to include audience Q&A whenever possible—ask your production team about audience interaction solutions such as Slido that can facilitate audience Q&A and live polling in non-interruptive ways to speaker and session.

4. Create a Memorable Experience That Puts Your Culture on Display

Another key principle of the B2H era is that customers, prospects, and yes, even event attendees do not check their humanity at the door before entering your conference venue. Within our personal lives, we look for opportunities to laugh and be entertained or to ask the deeper questions that inspire us to live for something greater than ourselves. Despite any dystopian criticism that may exist, business is fundamentally a human endeavor. Finding ways to appeal to that humanity at your conference, rather than planning that Airport Radisson seminar of years gone by, will contribute to building a memorable experience for attendees and put the best of your company culture on display.

One of our company values at Gainsight is "Childlike Joy"—the idea that we should aspire to bring that same limitless joy that children possess to our jobs every day. We've planted surprise moments at Pulse over the years to catch our audience off guard and delight them in the spirit of Childlike Joy. We've produced what is surely the only Customer Success musical theater performance inspired by Broadway and Disney. We branded our keynote stage as Central Perk from *Friends* and re-enacted a lost episode of the hit 1990s TV show using impersonators as actors. We hired a stand-up comedian to pretend to be the CFO of a publicly traded company and poke fun at the moderator (which, sidebar, accidentally offended the front row). We staged an impromptu audience sing-a-long by planting an a cappella group in the crowd who took to the stage to lead the audience in a rendition of "Shout." These are only a few of the moments we've created to inject humor and delight into the programming of our corporate event—moments that helped control energy that powered attention and information retention, create conversations that facilitated better networking among the attendees, and deliver a brand around our conference and community that makes Pulse so much more than just a business conference.

However, creating memorable experiences doesn't have to be musical theater and a cappella groups. Here is a list of things you can take into consideration to challenge the status quo of event planning and build an experience that will leave your audience talking:

- **Creative Venues.** If you're just starting out, or if the current size of your conference is modest, consider bucking the hotel and convention center trend and finding nontraditional venues to host your conference. Art galleries, sports arenas, or even historic venues such as libraries, gardens, and retired castles (yes, I've seen it done) could serve as unique environments that would make your program stand out from the pack.
- **Better Food.** While some venues have strict food and beverage (F&B) requirements, pushing back from the traditional buffets or boxed lunches can make a big impact on the event experience. Consider bringing gourmet food trucks to the

event venue or hiring a notable chef to create a custom menu. Just remember to account for all dietary restrictions by capturing those requirements on your event registration forms.

- **Convenience.** Large events, by nature, are inconvenient for things like charging your phone, finding a quiet place to take a call, or even hosting an impromptu meeting. Make it easier for your attendees by building dedicated spaces on the show floor that address all of the little things that they may need. We've made it a point to create dedicated spaces at our conferences for mother's rooms, prayer rooms, and even wellness areas to just get away from it all. Make sure the event Wi-Fi is strong and reliable, and you're guaranteed an extra +5 points on your post-conference NPS survey.

- **Themes.** Some companies decide to use themes as a way to brand the experience at their conferences—whether those themes are contextually relevant to their category positioning (the future of work, etc.) or just for fun (sports, music festivals, or nostalgic era themes). One of the best themes we've ever activated at Pulse was the 1990s, which included a surprise performance by Vanilla Ice, sliming our CEO on stage, and an incredible 1990s cover band that blew the roof off of our after-party.

Fortunately for event marketers tasked with figuring all of this out, planning a corporate event typically requires working with external agencies and vendors who do a lot of the heavy lifting. To create an incredible experience for attendees, choose partners carefully and don't trade off investments in quality AV production that can bring even the craziest ideas (see above) to life. Your partners will work with you to co-develop a show flow (or Q2Q) document that records even the smallest details in the sequence of your show and gets the entire team on the same page.

5. Use Pricing Tactics and Team Activations to Drive Registrations

You may wonder whether conferences subscribe to the adage popularized by 1989's *Field of Dreams*—"If you build it, they will come."

Table 8.1 Five Levers for Driving Conference Registration

Lever	Functional Owner	Intended Audience
Advertising	Marketing	Followers, Target Accounts
Database Emails	Marketing	Opt-In Audience
Outbound Cadences	Sales Development	Prospects from Target Accounts
Relationships	Sales, Customer Success	Active Pipeline, Customers
Influence	Executives, G&A	Investors, Analysts

Unfortunately for marketers that's not quite the case—driving registrations to your event takes a bit more effort than building a baseball diamond in a cornfield in Iowa. Table 8.1 highlights the five primary levers most effective in driving registrations for your conference when you're ready to launch.

With so many different functions on the hook to drive attendance, this is another example of how conferences truly become company-wide efforts. Marketing can play a central role in enabling each department (or frankly, employee) with promo codes, email templates, social images, and other assets to help amplify registration efforts. I've found that despite all efforts, however, the lion's share of registrations are driven by Marketing-led email campaigns to the marketable database. With that in mind, what kind of campaigns are effective?

It turns out that campaigns such as speaker announcements, general availability of the agenda, or any other aspect of show programming are great to create buzz for the conference and nurture your audience toward a decision—but there's only one type of campaign that actually convinces them to the point of swiping their corporate card: money. Messaging to your audience that a specific pricing band is set to expire, or pricing will increase on a given date, or that tickets are running out will move the needle in securing registrations. With that in mind, it's absolutely critical to develop a pricing strategy and promotional calendar in planning that optimizes around several urgent calls-to-action of price increases. As you build the financial model for the conference, arrive at a terminal revenue per attendee number that satisfies the budget and carve out Super Early Bird, Early Bird, and Advanced SKUs with discounts down to that terminal price per attendee. You'll find that honoring expired pricing or enabling your Sales Development, Sales, and Customer Success teams with promo codes to adjust pricing around the different bands can be effective motivators (and make your team look like heroes along the way).

Since industry conferences are primarily focused on best practices and networking, companies may be interested in sending several members of their team to the event rather than just signing up with a single ticket. In order to incentivize that behavior, event marketers can create team packages that both discount pricing by volume of registrations and provide experience boosters, such as dedicated meeting space onsite, conference swag, exclusive access, and educational resources. While prospective attendees have come to expect discounted registrations, some of the value-added activations that enhance the team's experience at the conference can profoundly impact the decision to transact. Many companies have dedicated budget for education and training that can be unlocked for conference attendance—building a program around this initiative and putting collateral into the hands of your field organization can result in dozens (if not hundreds) of registrations from a single account. As your category matures, the growth in conference attendance every year is a great proof point for the momentum behind your category and community, so being thoughtful about how you scale the registration effort is critical.

6. Monetize by Adding Value to the Prospect Experience

I opened this list of seven principles by convincing you that industry conferences are meant to be about the movement in your category and not about your company or products. That is indeed true; however, unless the conference *is your actual product*, you do have an underlying product or service that you intend to sell into the community you're creating. Striking the balance between building and monetizing community is tricky, but there are thoughtful ways that Sales, Marketing, and Customer Success teams can work together to drive business results by adding value to the prospect experience. Do this right, and your conference program can create, accelerate, and influence revenue unlike any other marketing program. Here are a few strategies that have proven successful for engaging prospects and customers at an industry conference and directly correlate to revenue impact:

- **Agree to Meet at the Conference.** One of the single most important metrics that we measure in our conference programs is the number of prospect and customer meetings that are both scheduled and conducted at the show. The asks are pretty straightforward for Sales and Customer Success teams, but for cold prospects, we coach our Sales Development reps (SDRs) to serve as concierges, offering up white glove service for our prospects, such as helping them plan the sessions they'd like to attend and facilitate any introductions on their behalf. This program gives our SDRs a reason to reach out to our registered database without compromising any trust as conference hosts.
- **Executive/VIP Dinners.** Marketing will assist in coordinating several executive dinners for the Sales and Customer Success organizations to engage executive buyers and influencers in a more intimate format. After a long day at the conference, executives would have benefited from seeing the brand on display throughout the day as category creator, industry thought leader, and community curator, setting a great tone for a more sales-oriented discussion over dinner.
- **Booth Presence in Expo Hall.** Most conferences require activating a partner ecosystem to help offset the expense of event production, a program that will typically include an expo hall filled with booths and buzzing with discussion. This is a space within the show floor dedicated to solicitation, and as

such, a perfect venue to exhibit as title sponsor of the conference and demo your products. While exhibitor booths will typically be turnkey and range in size based on level of investment and availability, ensure that your booth is custom and stands out from the others in size and scale.

- **Onsite Executive Briefing Center (EBC).** Dedicating real estate at your venue to host the meetings you scheduled leading up to the conference is a great idea, especially if you're able to build a branded space that can impress. These spaces should be designed as private meeting rooms, enabled with AV, and fully catered with water, tea, coffee, and healthy snacks throughout the day. Create a process for internal teams to book meeting rooms in advance in order to invest in a great experience for prospects and customers, and keep everyone on the same page logistically while at the show.

7. Measure Your Success

Make no mistake about it, conferences are a lot of work. But there is arguably no more effective weapon in the category creation arsenal than launching and scaling a conference program. In Chapter Twelve, I'll go into depth on the specific impact that conferences can have on company growth, but it's important to call out how to measure the success of the program itself. Here are a few metrics to consider:

- **Net Promoter Score (NPS).** Calculate your NPS by issuing a post-event survey to all attendees asking for an answer to a key question, using a 0–10 scale: How likely is it that you would recommend our conference to a friend or colleague? Respondents are grouped as follows:
  - "Promoters" (score 9–10) are loyal enthusiasts who will keep coming back to your conference.
  - "Passives" (score 7–8) are satisfied but unenthusiastic and vulnerable to competition.
  - "Detractors" (score 0–6) are unhappy attendees who can damage your brand through negative word-of-mouth.

Subtracting the percentage of Detractors from the percentage of Promoters yields the Net Promoter Score, which can range from a low of −100 (if every respondent is a Detractor) to a high of 100 (if every respondent is a Promoter).

- **Growth in Attendance.** Close the books on how many unique people attended your conference, what the registration-to-attendance ratio looks like, and how this year's performance stacks up against previous years. Again, for category creators, this metric shows up time and time again on investor and board slides as an indicator of the momentum behind your category.
- **Meetings and Impact to Pipeline.** Consider the number of meetings booked ahead of the conference and how many actually happened at the show. Segment the data by proving impact to sourcing net new pipeline and advancing existing pipeline.
- **Closed Revenue.** While this might be difficult to forecast immediately after the conference, continue to monitor the new business deals sourced and influenced at the conference, as well as impact to renewals/net retention and upsell/cross-sell revenue generated.

Beyond these metrics, conferences can impact your business in exciting and intangible ways that often don't show up in spreadsheets. Your customers at the conference will take great pride in being affiliated with the market leader. Your employees will leave hyper-motivated, knowing that they're contributing to something bigger than just the company. Your investors will leave confident in the bet they've made on you and your team.

By following these seven principles for planning an industry conference, your company can harness the most powerful part of category creation—growing a community of loyal brand advocates (whether they're customers or future customers) and helping them self-actualize within your category. These programs appeal to our basic human pursuit of belonging and, in turn, help build incredible affinity between the brand you're building and the people in the community you're leading.

9 | Activate Customers as Brand Ambassadors

One of the preconceived notions you might have first had when picking this book up is that companies create categories. I can understand why—almost every example I've shared so far attributes the success of a new category to a specific brand. The tactics that I've documented in this playbook are funded and operated by companies who aspire for category dominance. The truth is that there's a missing party in the narrative here who actually carries all of the leverage and authority to crown a category created—the customer. In the last chapter, I spoke at great length about how central community is to category creation—a vibrant ecosystem made up of customers, non-customers, partners, investors, and other constituencies external to your organization. At the end of the day, a company's ability to create a category successfully is inextricably linked to validation from its ecosystem—with customers serving as the most leveraged relationships from which to begin.

Consider a company that yells new category positioning into a void themselves with no external validation. Eventually, the company will realize that something isn't working with that approach and move on to try something new. But what if that same company created a platform for other voices to position the category, with trusted voices from reputable companies? Would that effort create a different outcome? The science says yes—that social proof is embedded in the psychology surrounding market perception of companies and their products. Dr. Robert Cialdini, bestselling author and career researcher of the science of influence names *consensus* as one of his six principles of persuasion—that people will look to the actions of others to determine their own. A recent survey by *Demand Gen Report* also revealed that "78% of buyers strongly agreed that they are placing a higher emphasis on the trustworthiness of content source, with 65% having higher preferences for content from industry influencers."[1] This doesn't suggest that your brand lacks credibility (even though it may in the early days), but customer validation will build and sustain trust and brand equity within your community in very profound and powerful ways.

As participants within your community, your customers are invested in your success. By becoming paid consumers of your products and services, they are literally betting on you to fulfill your vision for the category and emerge victorious as the market leader. This is an especially important observation in the early days when customers may make up the minority share of your community—they've arguably taken a bigger chance on you at that moment in time than several years and several hundred customers later. As you invest in their success, you'll notice that customers will actually *want* to advocate on your behalf—it's not a favor asked of them. Recall from Chapter Six that information, novelty, and status are the primary motivations of early adopters in new markets. Companies can create programs that appeal to all three motivators, finding opportunities at every corner to highlight the customer's greatness rather than their own. With that in mind, let's explore the different ways that customers create categories.

How Customers Create Categories

While there are entire industries and economies of people who do not yet appreciate your category, there is a small (but growing) audience

---

[1] "2018 Content Preferences Survey Report," *Demand Gen Report*, April 2018 https://www.demandgenreport.com/resources/research/2018-content-preferences-survey-report

of customers who do. These individuals will play an instrumental role validating your leadership and the category that you're creating by leasing you their brand equity. Now a lease is not forever. Later in the chapter we'll dive into what companies need to do in order to make customers successful, which, in turn, will fuel the advocacy motion for years to come. Here are a few tangible ways that customers can impact category creation.

1. Customers Validate the Pain You've Observed Is Real

One of the key tenets of category creation is discovering and popularizing an unmet need in the marketplace. Your content efforts can fuel popularization—recall that articulating the "why" ought to be one of the early focuses of your content marketing strategy. However, in order to truly drive resonance around the previously unrealized pain in the market, your company can't be the only one talking about it. Whether they react by amplifying your content on social media or respond by contributing content with their own points of view, hearing the stories from customers themselves will create a very important act of validation and halo effect around the category.

By participating in the conversation and, ideally, referring to the category by name, your customers are effectively telling the world that they themselves have felt the pain that you've observed, that the solution for that pain lies in embracing this new category, and that your company is leading the effort to eradicate the pain for everyone. Customers may even evangelize your product value as part of the overall solution which can help build brand equity and drive growth—a practice that ought to become operationalized as part of your Customer Marketing organization as time goes on. Their experiences matter, and in B2B, so do their job titles and company logos. The ability to orchestrate conversation through aspirational and leading brands in your industry will serve as a force multiplier for your validation efforts. If *Acme Corp* is talking about this category, maybe I should pay attention.

2. Customers Co-Author Industry Best Practices

With more companies now enrolled in the mission behind your category, these early customers are becoming the first few practitioners within the new discipline. Whether deploying and battle-testing some of the best practices that your company has published as part of your content marketing efforts, or blazing their own trail in operationalizing the discipline within their own businesses, customers are undoubtedly getting smarter about how to solve the problem that you've observed. It won't be uncommon for them to share what they're learning with their networks, but providing them with an opportunity to instead share their stories on your platform can provide mutual benefit. The customers themselves will benefit from your emerging brand and the promotional throughput that you'll leverage to drive visibility of the content. For your company, building a platform for the community to share their learnings with each other will both amplify your thought leadership as credible and contribute to your ongoing ownership of the conversation surrounding the category online.

The reality is that not one customer is the same as another. Each company that you sell to will likely look different—whether that's the size of the company, the industries and verticals they sell into, or even the geography in which they operate. Aspiring to create content to serve the entire potential of your market completely alone is a fool's errand. In fact, everything that you are learning and writing about as the category creators is somewhat nuanced relative to where you are in your own category and company maturity. You can't truly write the "how to" content for your category alone and without the support of the entire spectrum of your growing customer profiles. Imagine being a startup tackling a complex issue for large enterprises—you may observe how to best approach solving the problem, but you are not living that same pain in your business day-to-day. You'd be much more credible allowing customers to share their approach with the world instead—again ideally on your web properties. Your customers will push your thinking on how the category is evolving and will help educate you on where the innovation opportunities lie ahead.

3. Customers Make Your Product Better

Although having a 10x product is not a prerequisite to category creation, you certainly can't create a category without an actual product to sell into it. One of the outcomes of this whole thing is to sell enough of your product that you can monetize your leadership in the market and actually fulfill the purpose for your category that you've expressed in the first place. Who knows, you may even build an outlier, successful company along the way. To get there, your product must eventually become widely accepted as the de facto standard for success in the category. That's not to say there aren't other competitive products in the market—it's just that yours is better.

Customers are paid members of your community, and as such, will have expectations that go well beyond your general audience on how your product itself will enable them to realize the outcomes they were promised throughout the sales cycle. Creating channels by which customers can funnel in feedback to your product teams on their journey with your technology is likely the most powerful method for influencing a roadmap in the early days of a category. That's not to say that customer requirements should always supersede the vision of the company, but remember that not every company you'll market and sell to looks similar to your own. As customers get better with the discipline, they will get better at using your products too and will shape how they should evolve to truly lead the market.

4. Customers Crown the Category Leader

We will go into this topic in great depth in the next chapter, but while there's general consensus that companies don't create categories, there has been some debate on who within the ecosystem can actually crown a category leader. To this day, some people believe that industry analysts have that charter—and through their inquiries, briefings, and paid public speaking engagements can understand where new markets are forming and which companies are leading them. This research will ultimately manifest into a market map, or perhaps the hallowed two-by-two quadrant that summarizes the net effect of that research. Now you may perceive a bit of cheekiness in my tone here—I do believe that analysts play an incredibly important role in category creation and I'll defend that case in Chapter Ten. But I also believe that the world has changed since these institutions have been founded and, because of this, customers now have easy access to sharing their voice and publicizing their brand allegiances for all the world to see.

While some of that voice may show up in online review platforms, the broad theme behind the delivery vehicle is that customers are willing to go on the record publicly to cast their votes for the category leader. This can show up when customers will allow you to feature their logos on your company homepage, or agree to conduct a case study on the success they've realized with you and your products. Perhaps they'll agree to speak at your industry conference, sharing their stories and successes of their affiliation with your company in front of a compelling audience of peers. It's so important for companies in early markets to both deliver success for early customers, but also to create opportunities for them to advocate on your behalf as ambassadors of both your brand and the category at large. This effort can't start early enough in your company journey. Let's talk about the role that your company can play in enabling customers across these four critical validation activities.

How to Create and Identify Brand Advocates

Identifying advocates within your customer base is a critical step to activating them as brand ambassadors in the marketplace—but before they're willing to advocate, you'll need to make them successful with your products. This may not necessarily happen overnight, but eventually, one of Marketing's jobs becomes to celebrate the success that customers are realizing in the category and to position them within the growing industry as pioneers. For early stage startups, I've seen companies compensate some early customers with equity as advisors and evangelists for the brand—seasoned leaders from well respected companies who would be willing to go on record and advocate while the value on the product side is still being realized. That's proven to be a pretty good hack to gain instant advocacy and category validation in the early days while the product may still be immature relative to the vision the company is painting.

But for the rest of us, the art and science of making customers successful is a discipline called (drum roll) Customer Success. I know I'm biased as this is the category that Gainsight's been building for the past seven years, but the reality is that a focus on Customer Success will by its very nature create an army of willing advocates within your customer base. Since I've shared the official definition of Customer Success in the opening chapter, a simplified way to understand the concept is as an equation: $CS = CX + CO$, or Customer Success is equal to Customer Experience plus Customer Outcomes. Experiences are the sum of all the touch points that a customer can have with your company—from the initial conversation with a sales development rep, to the number of emails they receive from your company, and even to the speed of resolution time of the support tickets they've filed with you. Outcomes, on the other hand, are a shared (and documented) vision of the customer's goals for buying your product and what it will take to achieve them before, during, and after the sale. By focusing on these two initiatives, companies can build a Customer Success strategy that creates a passionate fan base of potential advocates and so much more. Figure 9.1 visualizes some of the prescriptive processes (which includes Advocate Engagement) that are based on hundreds of implementations and decades of experience in company-wide Customer Success at Gainsight.

Understanding that a well-executed Customer Success strategy will build advocacy is important, but getting started may sound incredibly daunting. Ultimately, founders and executive teams will need to appreciate that while customer success is a top-down, company-wide commitment, a dedicated Customer Success team will need to own the charter—a topic that deserves another book of its own (trust me, we've written it). But before you head to Amazon.com, I'll summarize nine steps for getting started with Customer Success today.

Figure 9.1 Gainsight's Prescriptive Framework for Cross-Functional Customer Success

1. **Define Success.** One of the biggest steps you can take to create a Customer Success–centric culture is to crystallize what success means for your customers. Many companies sell horizontal products that can be used in a variety of use cases. If you're a CEO or senior executive, you should kick off a cross-functional process to canonize the common use cases for your offering and define what success would mean to the customer in each of those use cases. A simple way to think about this: If you asked customers, "What does wild success with our company mean to you?" what would they say? Without defining the goal, it's hard to rally the company around it.

2. **Align Around Success.** Next, review your organization and make sure that each functional area knows what it must do to support Customer Success. Your CS team can be the quarterback of the initiative, but it needs buy-in from each department. This could mean reviewing CS feedback each month with the product team, defining and refining sales qualification criteria, or reviewing messaging regularly with the marketing and customer success teams.

3. **Listen to the Customer Success Team.** If you're a senior executive or CEO, you are likely flooded with signals about your business—from customers, partners, investors, and employees. You need to make sure a key part of that signal comes from the Customer Success team, since they are the eyes and ears of your customer base. Establish a regular review of Customer Success issues. Include a Customer Success executive in every executive meeting, every board meeting, and every key strategic decision. And take his or her opinions as seriously as you take those of your sales leader.

4. **Prioritize Customer Success.** This is where the rubber meets the road. Every business has limited resources and must make tradeoffs. Is the feature to delight clients always getting deprioritized for the feature to drive demos? Is the project to implement self-service getting pushed behind the channel

partner rollout? Is the training for Customer Success managers (CSMs) being postponed for the sales training? If you want to drive Customer Success, prioritize it.

5. **Empower the Customer Success Team.** In the same vein, if you've created a team to drive success with your customers, take measures to support it. Some things to consider:
   - Make sure the title for the Customer Success executive is on par with the sales leader.
   - Keep your CSM in the loop when a customer escalates to the management team.
   - Let the CSM be the hero with customers if possible (e.g., ideally the CSM will tell the customer that you agreed to their contract change or roadmap request).
   - Make it clear to the rest of the organization that the CSM represents the client's views.

6. **Measure Customer Success.** Customer Success will never be taken seriously if there aren't agreed upon metrics to apply. Define metrics for your bottom-line results, including gross churn, net retention, and other measures. Make sure everyone is clear on what the metrics mean. And create some early warning metrics such as health score, adoption score, and net promoter score (NPS) to track where customer success is going.

7. **Incent Toward Customer Success.** Companies set compensation plans to drive behavior. So if you want to drive Customer Success, pay people for it. Consider adding Customer Success metrics (e.g., net retention, NPS, or health score) to your company bonus plan.

8. **Challenge the Company.** Just as you push the company to grow sales and hit quarterly targets, expend as much effort pushing the company to hit Customer Success targets, such as retention, go-lives, satisfaction metrics, or adoption goals.

9. **Celebrate Success.** Customer Success isn't easy. It's not always in your control, and customers can be challenging. Most companies have great traditions for cheering sales on—gongs, champagne, trips, fun bets. Do the same for Customer Success.

Get yourself a CSM gong and send the signal that Customer Success is a top-down, company-wide commitment.

By building a Customer Success strategy, your company will unlock an exciting and powerful business lever that will drive sustainable growth through a variety of methods, including increased retention and expansion revenue. At the heart of it all is a customer who continues to realize positive outcomes with your company that's delivered in an intentional and delightful experience. For the marketers who are reading this, not only are these successful customers candidates for advocacy programs, but they will *want* to advocate on behalf of your brand. The next step is to create opportunities for them to do so.

How to Engage and Mobilize Advocates

If you're like me, asking people for favors can be a very uncomfortable experience. It's not that I can't benefit from the help, it's just in my nature to not want to inconvenience others for my own sake. That's why it took me a while to really appreciate that advocacy moments are not favors, but opportunities for customers, teammates, or general members of the community to go on the record with their personal stories and experiences. But understanding who should do the asking is an important discussion—typically the Customer Success team is closest to the customer and has the relationship, but marketers are the creatives with program and channel ownership on the other end of the ask. Each organization may have its own preferred process, but incentivizing the Customer Success team to identify potential advocates using health score data and enrolling them into a marketing-owned advocacy program has served us well over the years at Gainsight.

Advocates come in all sizes—senior executives from impressive logos whose endorsement carries high influence, to front-line practitioners who lean into your brand and are passionate users of your products. Both profiles are important. The upper quartile of titles may require a higher touch to manage—perhaps by forming a Customer Advisory Board or by leveraging and investing in an executive sponsor program—but offer significant value in terms of company and category validation and acceleration. Advocates further down the org chart can often provide deeper and far more hands-on perspective. Since it's likely the case that there are more practitioners than executives in your community, you also can benefit from the sheer breadth of the distribution value they bring to the table. There are some great technology platforms such as Influitive (a category creator in Advocate Marketing) that can help operationalize engagement for the long tail of advocates.

One way to spark the flywheel for your advocacy program is to incentivize participation or, said another way, to offer rewards in exchange for action. While this strategy may not sit well with some readers, the psychology behind most willing advocates is closely related to that of early adopters as described in Chapter Six. Information, novelty, and status are core motivational drivers for early adopters, but advocates take it a step further by valuing what Influitive refers to as access, power, and stuff.[2] *Access* means treating your customers as VIPs or rock stars, creating exclusive experiences such as a private networking event or customer-only lounge at your industry conference. *Power* creates a belief that advocates can actually influence the strategy of your business or category, through programs such as beta access to messaging or product releases in exchange for feedback. *Stuff* is a bit more material—perhaps gift cards or company swag—that will typically appeal more to the long tail of advocates. With the exception of the last category, you can see that incentives don't have to be gifts necessarily, but rather, opportunities to communicate appreciation for the vote of confidence given.

---

[2] Truman Tang, "Irresistible Incentives That Motivate and Engage Customer Advocates," Influitive, March 28, 2014, https://influitive.com/blog/incentives-customer-advocates/

With successful customers identified and the engagement mechanics we discussed in place, your advocates are ready to be mobilized. Present them with the right opportunities to create and contribute to the momentum of your category, and you'll have more than advocates but true *ambassadors* on the side of your brand. Earlier in the chapter, I discussed how customers create categories—by validating the pain observed in the category, co-authoring industry best practices, pushing the boundaries of your product development, and crowing industry leaders through words and actions. Table 9.1 explains how specific advocacy moments can map to the outcomes that category creators are intending to drive through their customers.

No person on earth has studied the power of advocacy in context of category creation more than Influitive CEO Mark Organ. I wrote about Mark in Chapter One; before founding Influitive, he was the founder and CEO of Eloqua—the creators of the Marketing Automation category. As a reminder, Eloqua had an incredible outcome by going public in 2012 before being acquired by Oracle later that year for $810M. One of Mark's greatest professional passions includes creating new billion-dollar categories, a topic he has graciously lent his deep experience to discussing in public forums and industry conferences. Now as a "second-timer" in category creation, Mark is driving the creation of customer-powered enterprises at Influitive, whose software and services help companies discover, nurture, and mobilize their advocates to accelerate sales and increase customer lifetime value. This practice, a new category called Advocate Marketing, creates an engaged customer community where advocates convert prospects into customers and new customers into successful customers. Mark was kind enough to share his learnings as a two-time category creator and specialist in the world of Advocate Marketing on how these two worlds converge for companies creating and operating in early markets.

Table 9.1   Understanding Advocacy Moments in Context of Outcomes

Outcome	Advocacy Moments
Customers Validate the Pain You've Observed Is Real	Early Stage Content Collaboration
	Online: blog posts, videos, e-books, podcasts, webinars, etc.
	Offline: speaking at events, etc.
	Press and Analysts
	Content and Program Amplification
Customers Co-Author Industry Best Practices	Early Stage Content Collaboration
	Online: blog posts, videos, e-books, podcasts, webinars, etc.
	Offline: speaking at events, etc.
	Press and Analysts
	Content and Program Amplification
Customers Make Your Product Better	Input on Messaging, Positioning, and Roadmap
	Customer Advisory Board
	Online Customer Community
	Roadmap Webinars
Customers Crown the Category Leader	Late Stage Content Collaboration
	Case Studies
	Testimonial Videos
	Quotes/Press Release
	Word-of-Mouth
	Reference Program
	Online Review Site Participation
	Social Media Engagement
	Referral Marketing

How to Activate Customers as Brand Ambassadors in New Categories
By Mark Organ, CEO and Founder, Influitive

The benefits of being the category leader are clear. The category leader in most cases is worth more than the entire previous category that it evolved from combined. Whether its Salesforce.com in cloud-based CRM versus all on-premise CRM solutions combined or Tesla in all-electric sedans versus all luxury sedans combined, the pattern is stable across markets and times. The company that has the best opportunity to become the category leader is the one that created the category in the first place.

While it is convenient and alliterative to discuss the notion of category "creation," in my experience that is not quite right. They are first category discoverers, and then popularizers.

Categories first exist in the minds of a group of enthusiasts who see the world differently from everyone else. These are the sorts of people who were bodybuilding with weights in the 1960s, building their own computers in the 1970s, connecting with each other over dial-up modems in the 1980s, purchasing goods and services online in 1993–1996, running their businesses using cloud-based software in 2000–2003, and utilizing influencers to market their businesses exclusively in 2010–2013. The category creator is first a category discoverer, identifying trends among these "freaks" who see the world so differently. Like anthropologists, they understand their mental models, to better serve them.

Anthony discusses the category of Customer Success in this book, a category that I believe will become a multi-billion-dollar

(continued)

How to Activate Customers as Brand Ambassadors in New Categories (*Cont'd*)

one in time. This category is built first upon the community of Customer Success professionals and leaders. When I was CEO of Eloqua, itself a category discoverer of cloud-based demand generation automation software (built upon a community of freakish demand gen professionals), we created one of the first Customer Success departments in 2002. As we were bootstrapped, holding on to every dollar of recurring revenue was mission critical. I was inspired by my work as a management consultant to generate strategic success with our product. There were a few lone voices in the wilderness discussing the need to both ensure that the SaaS product was adopted, as well as drive mission critical goals for companies—and they often put "success" into their titles. Both Salesforce.com and Eloqua called this emerging function "Customer Success" in 2002.

Once understood, the category is then popularized. The massive benefits of the new category is marketed so that more people are converted. If done well, and the underlying technological and other trends are strong, the "freaks" soon become the majority. The best way to popularize the category is with the very people who make up the community in the first place. After all, these people are trusted, use the right language, and are motivated to make the category as large as possible.

As Anthony discussed in Chapter Eight, the smart category creating company also organizes the category community. This can be done physically through conferences, local speaking events and dinners, and online through discussion and community software, public network community participation created on sites like LinkedIn and Facebook groups, and private messaging channels created on mobile technologies like Slack and WhatsApp.

The company should focus on marketing the category, while the community of company advocates should be the ones to evangelize the specific company and products. When we host dinner events for category participants and prospects at Influitive, the rule is that our executives can only discuss the food, wine, children, and hobbies. The selling is done by the happy customer advocates. They are much better at it than the executives, as they are trusted, use the right language, and are motivated. Category conferences that are well done follow a similar model. Gainsight's Pulse and Influitive's Advocamp conferences have their creators as primary sponsors and hosts, their logos barely visible. The message is that these events are focused on the needs of customer success and customer marketing professionals first.

When should the category creators organize their community? As soon as possible! The earlier the community is formed, the more likely a company is to glean the benefits of that community both for product development and for marketing. Carl Pei, founder of a category creating smartphone manufacturer, wanted to create a breakthrough in price and performance. A full year before creating a prototype, he created an online community of "smartphone nerds," who would debate various difficult product design decisions. When the OnePlus One was created, this same community felt a sense parenthood over the product and popularized it. The OnePlus One sold over $300M in its first year, and the company spent less than $3,000 on marketing; all the promotion was created organically in the OnePlus community.

The OnePlus example highlights the principles of what motivates the advocates of the category creator to apply their discretionary work effort on a company's behalf. Before I started Influitive, I interviewed hundreds of "super advocates"

(continued)

**How to Activate Customers as Brand Ambassadors
in New Categories (*Cont'd*)**

to understand their mental models and what it would require
for them to advocate even more than they already did. The
results of this research have created our framework for brand
ambassador mobilization:

1. **Exclusive Tribe.** Why do some people paint their
   faces and wear the colors when they attend their team's
   sporting events? Or tattoo the names of companies like
   "Harley-Davidson" on their bodies? People long to be
   part of something bigger than themselves, a movement, a
   religion they can believe in. They want to buy into a mis-
   sionary narrative. The Christian community has a powerful narrative of life after death. OnePlus catalyzed it's
   community with "Never Settle," a rallying cry that people
   deserve to have the best smartphone technology for the
   price of ordinary devices. Great category communities
   should have a distinct identity tied to a sense of purpose
   that encourages the missionaries to join and be active.

2. **Measurable Impact.** People perform more activity
   when they receive feedback on their contributions.
   Receiving variable rewards for activities is the principle
   by which slot machines, checking email, and scrolling
   through a social media feed is so addictive. Well-designed
   communities provide feedback to participants as to
   their effectiveness, whether it's the number of likes on
   a social media post, the audience ratings of their conference speech, or if the referral they provided has entered a
   demonstration stage and then closed.

3. **Social Capital.** When a community recognizes participants
   for the good work they have done inside the community,
   it feels great for the participants. But if by advocating for

a category and company, their career and life prospects improve, it can drive an obsessive level of activity. Providing awards, badges that can be displayed publicly on LinkedIn, and activities that are career boosters like speaking and writing opportunities all contribute to social capital.

These are the macro factors that drive community participation and advocacy over the long term. They are necessary but not sufficient for driving maximum engagement. Micro factors ensure that every session that an advocate has with your community increases the affiliation with your brand and inspires investment on their part. Removing the friction to advocate is just as important as increasing the rewards for doing so.

Video game designers have long figured this out, and ensure that users receive their "hit of dopamine" at the right times to increase their level of investment in the game. Smart marketers can leverage the same ideas. In both online and physical presence communities, small rewards—no more than tokens of appreciation—can be provided in exchange for activity. It's important that these rewards are not seen as pay for performance, but paying for their time. Virtual badges in online communities and lanyard pins at conferences provide valuable recognition but cost nothing. Access to exclusive content and networking also work in both the virtual and real worlds.

The category leaders of the future are more likely to be literally powered by the activities of their customers, which provide an irresistible drive to industry dominance. These companies have their customers participating in every aspect of the business, from product development to customer success, marketing to sales. When there is an army of unpaid but yet very effective people building a company, it is difficult not to win. In this way, the rewards to creating the category become so much better, when also investing in becoming customer powered.

10

Recognize That Analysts Don't Create Categories, Customers Do

Had this book been written only a few decades ago, it's likely that the entire 60,000+ word manuscript would have detailed a playbook for influencing industry analysts to recognize your new category. Ever since the rise of independent research and consulting firms in the mid-to-late 20th century, buyers at companies across major industries have looked to these organizations for research and advice on trends to pay attention to and which vendors were leading the markets behind those trends. Analysts have become such an important part of influencing market leadership and purchasing decisions that companies (especially in B2B) have built dedicated teams around an *analyst relations* function to ensure that their brand and value proposition were front of mind.

The Institute of Industry Analyst Relations (IIAR) defines an industry analyst as "a person, working individually or within a firm, whose business model incorporates creating and publishing research about, and advising on how, why, and where information and communications technology (ICT) related products and services can be procured, deployed, and used."[1] Typically each analyst firm will have their own set of services or offerings, but in general, the following activities are core to the business model for most:

- **Retainer or Subscription-Based Advisory.** Research access (typically incorporating an agenda), conference seats, and the right to speak to analysts for a certain amount of time. Access to analysts are typically referred to as *inquiries* and address any questions about published research.
- **Numbers and Research.** Data gathering and research services for either strategic planning purposes or content development aimed at an end-user audience.
- **Vendor Consulting.** An opportunity to update the firm about strategic developments such as new product releases or acquisitions—typically referred to as *briefings.* Note that in some cases, you do not need to be a paid customer of an analyst firm to conduct a briefing, as analyst participation is based on interest and availability.
- **Marketing and Opinion.** A number of "outbound" services that work in support of vendor marketing, including conferences, white paper production and delivery, and presentation and speaking opportunities.

The "gorilla" in the market is Gartner Inc., with annual revenues exceeding \$3.9B annually and over 15,000 customers around the world. As of 2013, more than 62% of revenue for the overall industry was attributed to the "buy-side" (end-users seeking advice) rather than "sell-side" analysts (vendors influencing the research). Analyst relations teams in most organizations spend their time building relationships with sell-side analysts through a combination of briefings, inquiries, and other engagement modalities, with hopes of influencing their research agendas. For market disruptors, this means showing up

---

[1] Caroline Dennington, "IIAR Best Practice Paper: Who are industry analysts and what do they do?" Institute of Industry Analyst Relations, August 27, 2013, http://analystrelations.org/2013/08/27/new-iiar-best-practice-primer-paper-who-are-industry-analysts-and-what-do-they-do/

favorably in research pertaining to the relevant category that they operate in. For category creators, this means being recognized in research as a credible market at all. While this practice is accepted and well understood today—the world is indeed starting to change.

How Customer Voice Is Challenging Industry Analysts

The rise of the Internet—particularly with the rampant popularity of social media—has given customers more voice than ever before. These media properties have given society permission and the enabling channels required to speak openly and freely on whatever comes to mind, without the need for a broker or intermediary. Surely there are damaging effects of dialogue when restricted to 280 characters or less, but on the more optimistic side, customers have ample opportunity to share their experiences with brands for all the world to see, whether positive or negative. We've seen evidence of this impact on our consumer lives—whether that's turning to Yelp over the Yellow Pages, or TripAdvisor instead of Frommer's to make decisions on places to shop or travel. Within our very humanity, we have changed the way we make considered purchases, giving more authority to the general populace than to the experts who weigh in from the sidelines. We look to our peers for information regarding the latest trends, who the trendsetters are, and how we can participate at the best price. This expectation is standard practice in our consumer lives, and it's starting to make its way into the office.

But even the most scathing customer opinion or review of an enterprise product never *really* made a dent in the success of that vendor. For decades, multi-year deals were struck between vendors and clients with the full contract value paid up-front. The vendor would then ship the product to the customer, and whether or not the customer ever plugged it in, the vendor would recognize that revenue and move on to the next sale. With a full assumption of good intent, customer voice *technically* did not matter to the financial success of the vendor until 45 to 60 days before that multi-year contract was up for renewal. At that point the phone call would come in, and the red carpet would be rolled out, only to find that the customer had never received value from the purchase in the first place and was already on to the next provider. That was the world we were living in, with customer success completely disconnected from business success, until the rise of the subscription and pay-per-consumption business models of the 21st century.

Today, customers have all of the power over vendors in the economic equation. Customers are far more educated about who you are, what you stand for, and the value of your products before they ever engage you in a sales cycle—having conducted their own research online and with what others have said about you. If customers are not realizing the outcomes desired with your products and services, or those outcomes have come at the cost of a great experience, they will churn and leave your brand for the competition. Beyond that, they will likely share their voices online and complete the circle, either contributing to the negative chatter about your brand or advocating on your behalf for all the world to see.

For the first time in history, customer voice is now inextricably linked to how businesses realize financial reward, and the pressure is on vendors to earn and maintain that trust. As that trend follows into the professional context from our consumer lives, customers are showing preference to turning to peers and trusted networks for advice on buying products rather than paying for brokered advice from the analyst community. It's not to say that this is happening at an absolute basis, or that industry analysts do not have their place in the modern world, but the level of transparency available for free online and completely absent from industry analyst processes is helping accelerate this transition. Beyond social media, online review platforms such as Capterra, G2, and TrustRadius have created a destination for this type of conversation, validating hundreds of thousands of user reviews to help professionals make smarter decisions about what software or services they buy. Customer voice is by far one of the most powerful forces of influence in early markets and, in my opinion, the right strategy to lean on in the early days of category creation.

The Challenge of Analyst Relations in Modern Category Creation

In Chapter Six, we explored the social psychology of early adopters and how category creators can harness their motivators of information, novelty, and status to capture interest and drive participation in the new category. Later, in Chapter Eight, we explored how the early days of new markets can be quite lonely for participants, who self-identify into a tribe and community bound by common cause in the purpose and vision articulated by the category leader. And finally, in the last chapter, we shared how making early customers successful with your products and services and then activating them as brand advocates and ambassadors can validate, define, and advance the interests of the new category. These forces all come together to give ultimate authority to customers—above anyone else—to dictate what is and is not a valid category.

One of the primary issues behind this trend is that analysts need to see a lot of dots in order to form a line. Most firms will only begin to pay attention to a trend once the volume of inquiries they receive on the buy-side becomes substantial. This pattern-matching principle leads analyst relations teams at vendors to influence on the sell-side by mobilizing several early customers to set up briefings with the firm. While this strategy may work well over the long run, it's very difficult in the early days of creating a new market. When you're in the early innings of creating a category, only you can see the line without all the connecting dots. You've observed the problem in the market before anyone else has, or at least are the first to popularize the problem you've discovered. Being first will require you to start connecting the dots on your category before any analyst can be helpful. It's a universal truth that's engineered into their business model.

Within the very first month of joining Gainsight, our CEO Nick signed contracts with two of the major analyst firms with the intention of getting help navigating how to position the company from trusted sources who understand the market. Looking back, Nick jokingly refers to that decision as "big company instinct," but the reality

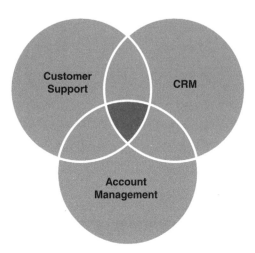

Figure 10.1 Analyst Impression of Gainsight Market Opportunity—January 2013

is that what the analysts told us—or didn't tell us—ultimately put us in a position to create a category around Customer Success. We got to work setting up briefings with our customers (all eight of them at the time), as well as conducting product demos of how our solution fit into the market that we saw developing. Once we shared the entire vision, we were surprised to see the feedback from both firms steer away from our vision and toward the research agenda already in flight (see Figure 10.1).

According to both firms, the best path forward would have been to position Gainsight as a proactive customer support solution, a next generation CRM (customer relationship management) provider, or even a platform for modern account management. Don't get me wrong: this advice was research-oriented, data-driven, and surely a viable option for our young business. However, it was not consistent with our vision, which we started developing more conviction for when we prioritized listening to our customers rather than the analysts. That conviction led us to a small, but passionate group of early adopters who carried the Customer Success job title, but no company in the industry was championing or paying attention to in a meaningful way. We became obsessed with finding ways to serve them, and in the process, developed the very philosophy and playbook contained in this book and the creation of a promising new profession and software category in Customer Success.

I would be remiss if I did not disclose that these were expensive contracts that we signed pretty early on in our company operations—years later, I wouldn't advise new startups to sign agreements with analyst firms right away. Remember that most firms will let you conduct briefings for free, which could be a worthwhile endeavor to better understand how these firms work. However, once you've made the decision to create a category, and perhaps forgone any analyst recommendations on positioning around an existing market, there are several ways to engage with them down the road in order to leverage their brand equity:

1. **Sponsored Research for Content Development.** As I mentioned earlier, certain firms will allow vendors to hire them in order to conduct research that can test a hypothesis in the market. That research will typically be output into a white paper, or other long form piece of content that the analyst firm will license for a fee. Oftentimes, they'll offer services that wrap around the research effort, such as hosting a webinar. Although these programs can often be quite expensive, they represent a direct way for vendors to influence analysts in order to create research under their brand surrounding the problem discovered in the new category. Promoting content that will bear the logo of a credible, third-party analyst firm that features your category name in the headline can be well worth the investment. One of the major firms that offers this service is Forrester Research, who calls the offering a "thought leadership paper" (TLP).

2. **Analyst Speaking Opportunities.** As you develop your event strategy—be it field events or industry conferences—analysts from tier-one firms are available for hire to speak to your audience. These programs are typically worth a look as an

extension of any sponsored research investments you've made with them, as the content will likely be far more impactful to your audience if led with data. Similar to the rationale behind sponsored content, having an analyst from a major firm speak at your events can add some credibility to your program, signaling to your community that the "mainstream research community is starting to pay attention to what we already know." If you're considering an analyst to speak at your conference, I would run their candidacy by the same speaking criteria that we discussed in Chapter Eight in order to ensure that both the quality of their presentation and their ability to deliver is high.

3. **Regular Cadence of Briefings and Inquiries.** Eventually, and only when your category starts to gain traction, it may be the time to start "playing the game" and develop a true analyst relations program. While having your category formally recognized on a Gartner Magic Quadrant or Forrester Wave will certainly be a company milestone worth celebrating, it is by no means the definitive proof point of a category created. But in order to build toward that milestone, companies need to prepare for the multi-year process of regular briefings with analysts on upcoming product releases, customer stories, positioning development, or any other relevant company updates that may impact the analyst research agenda. Remember too that firms will only pay attention to categories that have demonstrated volume of inquiries on the buy-side, so mobilizing your advocates to engage the analyst firms with inquiries about your category will certainly help your cause.

Analysts will ultimately be more helpful further into your company lifecycle once your category is more defined. Their influence can help potential customers make purchasing decisions within your category, especially if you sell to clients in the Fortune 1000 or where the deal structure is complex, changing, costly, or critical. But in the early years of category creation, your time is better spent with customers—although some of the lessons previously mentioned can be applied more broadly if we can expand the definition of analysts in the classical sense.

Expanding the Definition of "Analysts"

The muscle that a good analyst relations program will build for you is this idea of influencing the influencers—a notion that involves program building and regular engagement with individuals who can provide trusted third-party validation to their respective audiences that back your claims. In most cases these are either individuals within your customer base or extended members of your community who are not yet paying customers of your product. However, there are cases of individuals who will likely never be paying customers of your product but have a certain degree of influence in your young category. It's important to get them on your side. Here are the three types of analysts that may emerge throughout your category creation journey:

1. **The Subject Matter Expert.** Also regarded as "thought leaders," subject matter experts are independent bloggers or advocates who have developed some type of following that garners attention. They typically are not employed by any competitors and are seen as one of the first-movers in building community around the pains and needs of your market. You would likely engage with these individuals to market through them and to their following, as they typically will not charge you for an engagement (since they are usually willfully employed). Rather, they are more focused on growing their own sphere of influence and rising to the top as an independent, vendor-neutral player in the space.

2. **The Super Consultant.** Similar to a subject matter expert, super consultants are independents who have gained notoriety in your young market. Unlike them, however, they will charge

you for their services. These are the individuals who offer consulting services for speaking engagements, content partnerships, workshops, and other bespoke programs that focus on more than just amplification of your own content efforts. You may consider working with super consultants to add credibility to your cause, especially when the market has yet to tip toward our next class of analysts.

3. **The Majors.** These are the tier-one organizations that we've described at great length in this chapter. Working with any one of "the majors" means fighting for the support of the loudest voices in the industry.

At the end of the day, no voice will be more relevant or important to your success in category creation than the voice of your customer. Whether expressed in the traditional way and brokered through an analyst firm or delivered through modern and direct channels such as online review platforms, the vote of confidence delivered by customer voice is the final word on which categories are credible and which companies lead them.

One of the companies helping usher in this new era is G2, a real-time and unbiased user review platform that helps buyers objectively assess what is best for their businesses. G2 leverages more than 700,000 independent and authenticated user reviews read by more than three million buyers each month, bringing transparency to B2B buying—and changing the way decisions are made. I've asked Michael Fauscette, chief research officer at G2, to share his perspective on how categories are created in this new and transparent world where customer voice is king. As chief research officer, working with vendors on category definition and positioning is *literally* in his job description. Beyond that charter, Michael spent almost a decade at IDC (one of the majors) leading the enterprise software research group, where he helped companies navigate category positioning in the traditional sense. No one is more qualified than Michael to speak from experience—and from the other side—on how companies can maximize customer voice to create new categories.

Real-Time Taxonomy
By Michael Fauscette, Chief Research Officer at G2

For any company introducing a new product or service that needs the support of creating a new market or changing an existing market in any industry, the process can prove to be very difficult. Technology, particularly software, has unique attributes that makes it even more challenging than traditional industries, particularly in getting market validation and gaining credibility for the new offering. Keeping up with the rate of change in technology, which continues to accelerate at an exponential rate, is difficult for business users and leaders. This means that picking up signals of change and adapting categories to provide the best visibility to technology users requires a new, real-time approach. It's just too difficult to keep up in an inflexible and unadaptable system. To understand this, it's useful to look at the way traditional technology markets were defined and validated historically.

Traditional Market Validation

The foundation for how software markets are defined and tracked is loosely tied to activities that evolved over the past 45 or so years. Technology industry analysts, technology vendors, and traditional and online media provide the structure to the underlying taxonomy, a set of descriptions, required features, and interrelationships between categories. The technology analyst firms played the biggest role in tracking and updating the way the industry classifies its products and provides market validation. The big three legacy firms, Gartner, Forrester, and IDC, arguably carried the most weight in the general market, although there are even discrepancies and disagreements between them. The big three, and the rest of the industry analyst firms, use the taxonomy

(continued)

Real-Time Taxonomy (*Cont'd*)

system to advise both businesses and software vendors. They also use the taxonomy for other things like organizational structure (analysts by market), producing reports, particularly the "big" reports like the Gartner Magic Quadrant, Forrester Wave, IDC MarketScape, etc., and tracking revenue/market share. Because of the many uses of the taxonomy by analyst firms, particularly tracking revenue, which impacts market forecasts and market share (including historical market share), there is a great deal of resistance to change. In other words, the system has enough inertia that categories end up being fairly rigid and can't adapt to rapid market changes. The firms tend to wait on making changes to see how the category will evolve and only change when the market is mainstream. In this model, building a new category is not predictive of where the market is evolving, but instead it is a historical representation for where the market has been. That simply doesn't serve today's tech-hungry businesses that rely on innovation in technology for competitive advantage.

Vendors have an important role in changing and adding categories. Developing new types of software to address new business problems or solve old problems in new ways is the life blood of software companies, particularly startups. It is also the fuel for modernizing businesses and being competitive in a much more dynamic economy. The so-called digital transformation that businesses are facing has elevated the priority of a comprehensive technology strategy to underpin the business platform. Competition in all markets is much more intense than it has ever been, and looking for competitive advantage is often tied to new technologies. To thrive in this environment, for many companies, means building a business platform that is nimble and flexible to enable the business to adapt to changing market conditions in real time. Demand for technology that helps create a competitive edge has never been higher.

This market reality means that innovation in the software arena is at its highest, and opportunity for startups that can quickly create buzz around new or evolved technologies is massive. First- or second-mover advantage can be the difference between unicorn status and survival. The traditional approach to building a new category, or even changing an existing category so that the company's message can get to and resonate with businesses, can be frustratingly slow. Even getting the attention of key influencers who are associated with adjacent or similar technology categories can be extremely difficult. Analyst time is valuable and limited, which means that the firms prioritize their time carefully. The reality for early stage startups in new or evolving categories that would most benefit from the attention and validation of analysts is that doing paid engagements with many firms is just not in the budget. So how can technology vendors overcome the inertia of the conservative and rigid management of categories by traditional firms and get the market validation they need to get the attention of technology consumers?

Voice of the User
Like many things in our hyper-connected, rapidly changing business landscape today, it is time to take a different and more innovative approach to category/market validation. Providing the best possible experience around categorization of new and evolving technology has to be built in a way that it can capture and respond to changes at the same pace as the market. The Internet created many opportunities to innovate and create value. Those opportunities come with a large dose of disruption though, including creating a platform that gives voice to the consumer in ways never experienced in the past. This change

(continued)

Real-Time Taxonomy (*Cont'd*)

was evident first in the business to consumer industries with the evolution of review platforms like Yelp and TripAdvisor, and the explosion of marketplaces like eBay and Amazon, which rely heavily on peer reviews to create trust online. The consumer use of peer reviews to guide all sorts of buying decisions has spilled over to business-to-business buying activities as well. People want and need to get validation from businesses and individuals that are similar to them, and share similar problems. We generally refer to this as the "like me" syndrome. It really is an extension of peer networks, which exist both on and off line, and have grown in reach and importance with the availability of online social networks like LinkedIn and Twitter.

Using review data to help support data driven decision processes for purchasing business technology is a fairly new phenomenon. Over the past several years the number of sites has increased and some of these sites have rapidly gained scale and, subsequently, influence with businesses. The sites vary greatly though in business model and quality of data. Many of the sites have business models that are very similar to free consumer sites that use the site traffic (and visitor data) to fuel opportunities for paid search placement and demand generation for technology vendors. These sites tend to focus more on content marketing and simple reviews to keep the traffic flowing and the experience for reviewers as frictionless as possible to maximize the opportunity for converting the visitor to a lead that can be monetized quickly. The sites that operate in that model are great for exposure and demand generation but not as useful for market validation and for generating data and research to help support the emerging category. A smaller number of B2B peer review sites, like G2, have a different business model that has an underlying double-ended marketplace platform and focuses on more detailed and highly vetted reviews that provide much more detailed insights into the use of the software and the problems that it solves. Sites in this model collect and use a broad data set to support both buyers of technology and the companies that create the tech. Their business model has some similarities to the traditional analyst firms, although driven by the voice of the user, and with opportunity to be much more flexible and adaptable with the underlying taxonomy.

A site like G2, to use an example I'm most familiar with, has nearly 90,000 products and services classified from over 40,000 vendors in over 1,500 categories. Both products and categories continue to rapidly increase as new products emerge, and global expansion means connecting and collecting data on regional and local software and services providers. For example, G2 grew the number of products on the site 95% from March 2018 to March 2019. The more diverse the business audience in industry and geography, the more data is needed to support the buyers visiting the site and doing research on solutions. If you compare that to a traditional firm like Gartner, analysts there track only 1,100 vendors in 400 categories (markets). Approaching and engaging with a research platform that has broad reach across diverse technology categories and with the desire to provide the most detailed and helpful information to buyers of technology provides the highest probability of getting early market validation. Today the voice of the user is the loudest and most influential to buyers. In a recent survey (G2, April 2019, N=1362), 82% of the respondents reported that they use online review sites for gathering information and getting recommendations and referrals for business products and/or services that interest them.

(continued)

Real-Time Taxonomy (*Cont'd*)

Real Time Taxonomy

The real time taxonomy that G2 developed and manages can change in a few ways. These include:

- Adding a new category.
- Evolving from a single category into sub-category/categories.
- Consolidating two or more categories into a single category.

The addition of a new category is triggered in a few ways. Often the initial conversation is initiated by an inquiry from a vendor that is trying to create the new category directly. There are also market changes that can lead to identification of the changing category, and sometimes the inquiries from buyers researching on the site will signal the developing new category. To accelerate the development of a new category, the following can help:

- List of business problems that the new category addresses.
- List of competitors in the market. To establish a category it's preferred to have at least six vendors, but 10 is the optimum number. That can be difficult in a new category, of course, so a list of all the companies that the vendor is competing against for business, even if the approach to the solution is a little different, is a good start.
- List of defining features that make the category unique from what came before.

Once the information is provided and evaluated successfully, the new category is created. Robotic process automation (RPA) software is an example of a new category that emerged last year. At times the initial discussion might lead to the need for more information, or even a demonstration of the software to provide the best possible definitions and understanding of the new technology. Sometimes, after the complete evaluation, the product may be assigned to an existing category that accurately represents the market at its current state of maturity.

The evolution of a category is a very common way that new categories are created. Business requirements might change, which drives to new features, or innovations might lead to a new way to address the problem. The original category might become the parent category of several new categories or might be broken out into several categories, replacing the original. A recent example will make this process clearer. In the content marketing category, which was created a few years ago, the products evolved to have many new features. The features though were not included in every product in the category, but instead reasonably distinct groupings of features emerged with products that did some but not all of the original category features. The original category of content marketing became three categories: content creation software, content distribution software, and content experience software.

Category consolidation is less common than the other ways the taxonomy changes. It often is more of the merging of features in some of the products in a category that leads to the creation of a compound product containing a mix of features across several existing categories. The best examples of these are "all-in-one" categories like CRM.

Engaging with a B2B peer review platform can help give new, innovative products a faster way to gain market validation. Generally you can start to work with the platform by working through a straightforward set of steps including:

- **Claiming your profile.** Since most platforms operate in a freemium business model, you can usually claim your

(continued)

Real-Time Taxonomy (*Cont'd*)

product profile for no cost. If the product isn't already listed on the site, you simply submit it on the front end of the site. Once it's submitted you can expect it to be added very quickly, although its initial category may not be what you desire, which leads you to the process outlined previously.

- **Upgrading the profile.** Upgrading the product profile page(s) (and on some sites a vendor profile as well) to some sort of subscription package will usually allow much more flexibility to create a profile that matches your brand and may even allow some content marketing efforts on your part, within some guidelines. The upgraded packages often include other marketing opportunities, from using research comparison reports for marketing to gaining access to different types of data and research to help improve the product and use to enable your sales efforts.

Gaining market validation using a real-time taxonomy with flexible categories is a faster route to market success. It is also much simpler to manage and will yield other assets that incorporate the most powerful market validation, the voice of the user.

11 | Establish Trust at Scale Through Authentic Executive Communication

Imagine that you're browsing your social feed when you discover a video of someone you recognize participating in a Carpool Karaoke sing-along stunt, similar perhaps to something you'd find on late night television. They're not celebrities or really famous in any way, but the production quality makes the two-minute video well worth the watch. Months later, you find video footage of that same individual in a recording studio working on a hip-hop single. You know he's particularly musically talented, but somehow you can't stop yourself from searching for the song on Spotify to hear what it's all about. Not bad, surprisingly. A few weeks later, you're at a corporate event where that same person—now somewhat more recognizable after having put himself out there—is pouring his heart out in front of an audience of thousands, sharing his struggles with loneliness and how that's impacted him both professionally and personally. Who *is* this person, and better yet, why are you so drawn to him? He's not an actor, musician, or any hired gun really.

For the marketers reading, what if I told you that that vulnerable, self-deprecating person on camera and on stage was your CEO? Founders and executives, what if that person was *you*?

I can appreciate that your first reaction may be that there's no way you'll ever get me (or my CEO) to sing along to Abba or Backstreet Boys on camera while driving through Palo Alto. You may also question the need for a chief executive to open up about personal struggles with mental health and be vulnerable in front of a professional audience of prospects, customers, partners, and analysts. But the truth is that these examples are not fabricated, but actual programs that we've challenged our CEO at Gainsight, Nick Mehta, to participate in. His courage and willingness to put himself out there has helped us communicate our company values and unique culture to the world, while positioning both Nick and the overall Gainsight brand as market leaders. Being able to run this play at scale is a "superpower" for companies who are creating new categories.

In the business-to-human (B2H) world in which we are now living, your executive team is on the record as official spokespeople for the business, or said another way, outward expressions of your company purpose, values, and culture. There's no getting around that—customers are interested in doing business with brands that they admire, and as we discussed in Chapter Five, would be very willing to change vendors to better align their own personal sense of purpose and values with the products and services that they purchase. Today, brand is inextricably tied to people, and your executive team plays a critical role in representing the faces and stories of the people at your company and in your community. This is especially important in category creation, where tribes and communities of people who are brought together by common purpose will always look to a leader for inspiration on the path forward. As the CEO of a company that's creating a category, that responsibility falls on you to authentically position yourself to the market at large as purpose-driven, an expert in your domain, and above all, human.

This process isn't exactly comfortable for most executives, or perhaps it's a lot more comfortable to be authentic and vulnerable in a small group setting. That's where marketing can help—capturing the authentic voice of the executive spokespeople and providing opportunities to deliver that message at scale through a practice known as executive communications or "exec comms." The trust that executives can establish by being their authentic selves in more intimate settings is a powerful lever for any business, but layering an exec comms strategy on top to establish that trust at scale is what makes the strategy a superpower. Your executive team can't possibly be everywhere at all times, but well-developed marketing programs can aid the effort of establishing trust and brand affinity with the market at large.

Marketing's Role in Executive Communications

Exec comms programs have typically lived within the public relations (PR) or corporate communications function—viewed as an extension of company effort to expose its executives to journalists and the media, speak at events, or even address important topics with investors or analysts. But PR and corporate communications are being reinvented in today's digitally connected world, as is the exec comms discipline. It will be just as important to position executives as category ambassadors to the media as it will be to teammates, customers, the community, and the market at large. As I discussed in Chapter Seven, the cost and level of effort required to produce high-quality content has dropped significantly, pushing ownership of the exec comms strategy somewhere between the communications and corporate marketing (or brand) teams.

Wherever the function lives, and whoever gets the charter, Marketing will undoubtedly play a key role in coaching executive spokespeople and expressing their authenticity through programs that your intended audience can relate to. Julie Ogilvie, a research director at SiriusDecisions, developed a framework for marketers building a program around what she defines as the four Cs of exec comms:[1]

- **Comfort.** Julie explains that one of the most important roles that marketing can play in exec comms is to help the executive

---

[1] Julie Ogilvie, "The Four Cs of Effective Executive Communications," SiriusDecisions, March 28, 2017, https://www.siriusdecisions.com/blog /thefourcsofeffectiveexecutivecommunications

relax and feel comfortable in the inherently stressful role of a spokesperson or public speaker. Creating simulated environments, such as media training, can reduce jitters and help executives become aware of what they are projecting through their voice and gestures while in a supportive environment. A good PR agency will typically offer media training or public speaking services to help facilitate this program.

- **Context.** With time scarce for executive teams, making sure they are prepared and understand the situation they are walking into is critical. Julie explains that one way to do that is to align "multiple executives with specific messages [that] grows your bench of speakers, and people are more likely to excel when they are talking about topics where they have significant knowledge." One of the companies that does a great job of this is Salesforce, who have many spokespeople each aligned to a specific set of messages. You'll observe that while Marc Benioff is the co-CEO of the company, he'll typically defer most of the business operations messages to his counterpart Keith Block, while Marc sets the vision for the category, the role that Salesforce plays in being a corporate citizen and force for change, and the importance of equality and trust in achieving those outcomes.

- **Content.** Marketers play a key role in developing concise content and talking points that can be delivered in a way that feels natural to the executive. Julie advises that "to do this effectively, executive communications people must be connected with the organization's content factory—and look for opportunities to adapt messaging for the executive's platform." This is especially important for category creators, because the content can in some cases have little to do with your company or products. Your executive spokespeople will play an important role in advocating for the category itself—selling those who are yet to believe on why it's important, and engaging those who already believe with resources and anecdotes on where the category is headed.

- **Connection.** Storytelling is such an important part of building an authentic connection between your executives and their audience. As marketers, Julie believes that "understanding their background and personal life—where they grew up, challenges they faced, their family situation—all of these things can contribute to a personal narrative that can underscore a business point." Transparency and vulnerability are such powerful tenets of storytelling, and when communicated in context of the business narrative, can establish trust with your teammates, customers and category at large.

Perhaps there's a fifth C to add to Julie's list—*culture*. As we discussed in Chapter Five, the very framework of creating a category is dependent on being able to establish company purpose (informed by the personal purpose of the executive team) and then to live that very purpose out loud. That purpose is often expressed through company values and result in a company culture that the category itself can take on as its own. Within an exec comms program, it's important to keep culture at the very core of every opportunity that an executive may have to represent the company externally—whether in media or a brand campaign. It's also important that it's delivered in a way that's authentic to the executive. At Gainsight, one of our company values is "childlike joy," this idea of bringing your inner child to work every day. For us, and for Nick especially, campaigns such as Carpool Karaoke or a self-deprecating rap performance felt authentic to who we are. Somewhat *silly* programs like these will not be appropriate for every brand or executive team, but what matters is finding your voice that *is* authentic to who you are and what you stand for. Authenticity, in whatever form it may take, is the most effective strategy in establishing trust and building market leadership in your new category.

The Importance of Establishing Trust in Category Creation

One of the most prolific voices on the role of leadership in category creation is Keith Krach. If you look him up on LinkedIn, his headline currently reads chairman and CEO of Ariba and DocuSign—the latter of which is a company he took public in 2018 that's now trading at a $9.4B market cap. But even a title that prestigious sells Krach short. He's also a mentor, leader, philanthropist, public servant, educator, and what he'll admit to being most proud of—a loving son, brother, husband, and father. One title most applicable to this chapter was "Category Kingmaker," a moniker given to him by *Profile Magazine* in 2017. Krach has been able to successfully create, and dominate, *four* separate categories:

- **Robotics.** GMF Robotics Corp, a joint venture between General Motors Corp. and Fanuc, Ltd.
- **Mechanical Design Synthesis.** Rasna (Acquired by PTC–1995–$180M)
- **B2B e-Commerce.** Ariba ($4B IPO in 1999, acquired by SAP–2012–$4.3B)
- **Digital Transaction Management.** DocuSign (IPO in 2018, $DOCU–$9.4B)

Krach certainly has developed his own playbook for how to create new categories, but he would be the first to tell you that at the core of the strategy is developing a values based leadership framework in an effort to establish trust with your new market.

Krach believes that building trusted relationships is at the very heart of creating a great category, a generational company, or even simply selling your product. If you boil down the strategies that we've explained in this book so far, the common refrain is that people will ultimately choose to give you their business *because they trust you.* Teams across your organization have to become extremely good at building trusted relationships—whether you're a front-line sales development rep (SDR) talking to a prospect for the very first time or a QA engineer validating the performance of the latest product release. Trust is typically built on a 1:1 basis, such as visiting a customer onsite, hosting a marketing event out in the field, or taking that red-eye flight only to shake the hand of a key decision maker for a big deal that may close this quarter. Those are trust-building activities, but as Krach puts it, everything in business is divided by time. Even the most self-sacrificial CEOs will need to enforce personal boundaries in order to prioritize time with family and loved ones. Even if they do not, there will never be enough hours in the day for them to maximize trust-building activities with the market, while also balancing the competing priorities of running the business itself. So how can you scale trust-building activities on a one-to-many basis?

Krach believes that the most effective form of leadership and trust building is authenticity—a virtue that Marketing cannot necessarily develop on behalf of the executive team, but can certainly amplify. All humans are endowed with our own unique set of talents, gifts, and core competencies, and great leaders are able to put down their guard and be vulnerable enough to share their authentic selves with the world. While for some of us being vulnerable is much easier in a 1:1 environment, Krach encourages leaders not to be afraid to be vulnerable on stage or in front of a camera. Your teammates, customers, and extended members of your community want to get to know the people behind the brand leading the category. What do they stand for, what's their background, what do they sound like? Ultimately, you'll be hard-pressed to find a wrong answer to any of the questions above, so long as you are authentic to who you are. Authenticity also means admitting on the record that not everything is as perfect as it may seem—admitting your fears or flaws or offering up a transparent perspective on the business. This means being transparent about more than just work, but also the appropriate parts of your personal life as well. If reality television and social media have taught us anything, it's that there's a market of people who are interested in *following* the lives of people they admire. We've all experienced the dark side of this trend—how social media will typically paint lives through rose-colored glasses. However, offering your community an authentic window into who you are inside and outside of the office can establish trust with the market in incredibly powerful and profound ways.

Being authentic means taking a step of courage, but when done right, can fuel your ability to establish trust at scale. That's where Marketing steps in—turning courage into a superpower for your brand.

How Marketing Can Scale Trust in New Categories

There are several channels by which marketers can amplify the authenticity of their executive team in order to establish trust with the market at scale. While these channels are often owned by different sub-departments within Marketing, it will be important to have someone (likely in Comms) own the overall strategy and editorial calendar on behalf of each executive spokesperson. Teams need to ensure that the specific messages and narratives that are aligned to each executive are consistent across each of the channels below— whether personal or professional.

- **Contributed Articles.** While journalists will often look for executives to comment or weigh in on a specific topic that they're covering, many high authority publications will also accept full-length articles as contributions to their website. While some publications will treat this as a "pay-for-play" opportunity, many of the tier-one outlets such as *Entrepreneur, Forbes, Fortune*, and *Inc.* are willing to read proposals for article contributions. Contributed articles are great channels for establishing trust by allowing executive spokespeople to write opinion pieces in their own voices, leveraging the viewership and promotional throughput that many of those publications possess to drive engagement. From an SEO perspective, inserting back-links to your homepage will improve search performance in your category, as the search authority of tier-one media publications will usually outweigh your own. It's important to understand the individual submission criteria of each publication and, from a narrative perspective, which stories are best aligned with their editorial direction.
- **Social Media.** The individual social media profiles of your executive spokespeople are important properties to develop and maintain. As vain as it may sound, an executive with a massive following on different social media platforms is a competitive advantage and a great opportunity to drive awareness and influence the market that you're building. Especially within the B2B context, Twitter and LinkedIn are two of the more important networks for executive teams to engage their audience and participate in conversations that surround the category. These networks provide great opportunities for executives to ask questions that engage their audience for feedback,

or as distribution channels for important pieces of content. Since executives are humans too (surprise!), you may consider maintaining personal profiles on Facebook, Instagram, or other consumer-oriented networks to facilitate connection on that front. Deciding whether or not to keep those accounts private or open to the community is a matter of personal preference. Don't fret if your executives do not have a strong initial following—building the right type of followership takes time and a tricky combination of promoting your handles and, more importantly, having something valuable to say on the platforms.

- **Speaking at Events.** As your category matures, your executive teams will be in high demand to speak at events and share their industry perspectives with curated audiences. These events may be programs you yourselves own (such as a field event or an industry conference that you produce), but on a volume basis, most speaking requests are sourced from outside the organization. Your executives may be asked to speak at third-party trade shows, company kickoffs, investor events, or perhaps even directly with media either on camera or in print. These opportunities should always be considered, as they'll help develop the professional brand of your executive team as leaders in the category, but also prioritized as volume will eventually outgrow bandwidth. This is why Julie Ogilvie's point from earlier in the chapter of developing a deep bench of company spokespeople can help scale your coverage and ensure your brand is present wherever conversation of your category may take place.

- **Brand Campaigns.** As I covered in Chapter Seven, the cost to produce high-quality audio and video content has dropped dramatically, giving marketers an opportunity like never before to give a face to your company and category. Consider using video programs that allow your executive spokespeople to speak directly to your audience—whether that's a quick iPhone video on LinkedIn sharing a quick learning from a customer meeting, or a more involved brand campaign (such as Carpool Karaoke) that allows your executives to put your culture on display. These programs can often appeal to our very humanity, creating a sense of connection with a market that is growing faster than our own ability to engage on an individual basis.

Developing an executive communications strategy, along with measured execution on the six other principles I've shared in this section, will put your company in a position to create and dominate a new market category. Whether you're starting this journey from step one, or are an established brand looking to break through a crowded market, the tactics I've shared will serve you well. Along the way, you will have built a human first brand that investors value over market disruptors in their portfolios, customers bet their careers on, and teammates feel inspired to be a part of. But how exactly does category creation correlate to the growth metrics that your CFO and investors are asking about? What are the implications of category creation on teammate retention and satisfaction? Can creating a category deliver a level of customer satisfaction greater than that of disruption-oriented companies? Let's unpack these three topics and prove the impact of category creation as we transition to the final section of the book.

Proving the Impact of Category Creation on Customers, Investors, and Employees

12 | How to Connect Category Creation Programs to Growth for Executives and Investors

Iconic theoretical physicist Albert Einstein once said that "not everything that can be counted counts, and not everything that counts can be counted." There's freedom in that quote for marketers—a business discipline that lives under constant pressure to prove the impact of their investments on business outcomes such as pipeline creation and revenue growth. While brand programs may be more difficult to quantify or attribute (at least directly) to growth relative to more traditional demand generation programs, a CFO or board member won't accept an Einstein reference as an excuse. The reality is that brand marketing efforts *do indeed* drive growth, and getting your executive team and investors to understand how these efforts correlate to revenue is critical to both cross-functional alignment on vision and securing the investment required to execute a category creation strategy successfully.

Proving the value of brand on growth is hard enough; however, as I described in Chapter Three, it's an even more difficult exercise for category creators. Recall the **two funnel effect**—this idea of a chasm existing in the market between interest in the category (funnel one) and interest in your products (funnel two). Success in funnel one means broad category awareness, identification of your company brand as a contributor to the discussion within the new category, and ongoing engagement around the best practices and resources that your team produces. Success in funnel two means hypergrowth. The momentum behind the first funnel must eventually correlate to momentum in the second funnel, otherwise, an observer may be right to question whether there's a real business to be built (beyond perhaps a media company) in your category. It may take some time, and benchmarking funnel performance against disruption-oriented companies may prove to be misleading, which can explain why only the long-term greedy have the patience to create a category.

But we know that successfully creating and dominating a category will lead to more sustainable shareholder value creation than almost any other strategy, on the magnitude of 53% incremental revenue growth and 74% incremental market capitalization growth, according to *Harvard Business Review*.[1] That upside is certainly worth the effort, but creating a common language and orientation around data is a necessary step to prove correlation and build the repeatable processes required to create and scale a generational company. In this chapter, we'll walk through the different growth outcomes that category creation can impact, empowering you with a language to speak to the value you are creating within the business in terms that a CFO or investor would appreciate. Ultimately, you'll be hard-pressed to convince anyone that category creation is working unless you can tie performance back to the funnel. However, before we get there, I want to introduce a series of phrases and acronyms that we'll use throughout the chapter to refer to various funnel stages. The stage names and definitions in Table 12.1 might be slightly different from how your company thinks about the funnel, but in general, should be fairly close to best practice.

---

[1] Eddie Yoon and Linda Deeken, "Why It Pays to Be a Category Creator," *Harvard Business Review*, March 2013, https://hbr.org/2013/03/why-it-pays-to-be-a -category-creator

Table 12.1   Funnel Stage Names and Definitions

Funnel Stage	Definition
Conversions	Conversions are individuals who have decided to visit one of your web properties and identify themselves to your brand in exchange for information. Each conversion is someone new to your marketable database. Consider an example where an unknown person visits Google and searches "VP Customer Success job description." She lands on a Gainsight blog post that has a sidebar element for a download. She enters her name and email address to get access to the content—signaling that she is interested in learning more about the thought leadership you are providing (funnel one).
Marketing Qualified Leads (MQLs)	MQLs are conversions who are signaling buying intent—typically this means interest in your products or services (funnel two). This can occur from a drip sequence, form checkbox, request a demo button, direct response PPC (pay-per-click) ad, or if a behavioral activity has pushed his lead score over the threshold for an MQL. In this case it's important to remember that a contact could be both a conversion and an MQL at the exact same time—for example, imagine an unknown person clicking on a PPC ad and landing on a page where the CTA is to request a demo and he completes the form. If that is the first contact that we have ever had with that person, he would be a conversion, but also an MQL.
Sales Qualified Leads (SQLs)	SQLs are MQLs that some qualification team—typically Sales Development or *SDRs*—decides are ready for an account executive (AE) to engage. These teams are operating on an agreed-on set of qualification criteria in order to determine which contacts are actively in market for your products and are willing to take a meeting with a sales professional. If an MQL gets thrown out and never becomes an SQL, that doesn't mean they shouldn't be marketed to; it simply means she isn't yet ready for sales. We'll talk about what to do with those folks later on in the chapter.

(continued)

Table 12.1   Funnel Stage Names and Definitions (*Cont'd*)

Funnel Stage	Definition
Sales Accepted Leads (SALs)	SALs are SQLs that are "accepted" by AEs and are considered active sales opportunities in the pipeline. There are a countless number of sales processes that companies can implement to progress SALs from early stage pipeline to late, and finally to "Closed Won" revenue—each methodology with its own merits. Marketing's job is not done when the opportunity is created, especially in new categories where prescriptive education on how to think about purchasing and deploying new products is critical to doing deals.
Closed Won	A signed contract! Congratulations, you've successfully brought a new customer on board or have closed a renewal or expansion opportunity with an existing customer.

The list in Table 12.1 is far from complete—most notably absent are the various sales stages that make up early- and late-stage pipeline between the SAL stage and Closed Won. However, each of the seven strategies that I introduced in Part II will ultimately impact growth outcomes that show up in the stages described here—but let's talk about how.

Six Growth Outcomes Impacted by Category Creation

Category creation is both a company-wide philosophy and marketing practice, but as we've discussed throughout the book, many of the programs in the playbook overlap with traditional marketing principles—just expressed through the lens of category creation. Therefore, all of the universally accepted growth outcomes that CFOs and investors care about for any business are relevant and directly impacted by a category creation strategy. Here are six examples of those outcomes and how to set expectations across the business on the impact of category creation:

1. Marketable Database Growth

Building and maintaining an opt-in marketing database of prospects and customers is at the heart of the modern marketing organization. Nearly all campaigns—whether content launches, event promotions, or personalized nurture—leverage email as a function of driving engagement. If your database is small or unfocused, you won't have an audience size large enough to drive the growth that your company desires. If your database is disengaged, or worse, spammed, your audience will unsubscribe. Therefore, the health of your marketable database is a reflection of the health of your marketing strategy. Building your database typically comes from either organic or paid media efforts at the very top of the funnel. For category creators, creating enough early stage content that's SEO friendly around the search terms relevant to your category is the best way to drive organic value. Over time, the organic effort will influence search volume on your company and category brand, which can be measured using the free Google Trends utility. Some companies will allocate budget to syndicate their content across high authority web properties, or pay advertising services to help drive more engagement with their content from their target audience. There are many leading indicators to account for the successful execution of organic and paid strategies, but ultimately, the number of conversions your team is able to generate is the appropriate lagging indicator. Are you getting the right persons opting into your database? Are they coming from the right company profile?

Conversions are the right metric to use in order to quantify the impact of brand awareness of your new category (funnel one), as well as a leading indicator into future sales (funnel two) given the campaigns that will be driven into your database. The gross number in aggregate is interesting, but reporting on conversions by demographic considerations such as persona, company size, or industry vertical can lead to important revelations that can inform your go-to-market approach in your new category. As an example, are SMB companies gravitating to the messaging that you're putting out in the market-place more than large enterprises? Are you finding strong resonance with director-level and below titles rather than above the line decision makers? Educating your executive team on how to think about conversions is bigger than the health of your database, but an early indicator on the health of your entire category.

2. Marketing Database Engagement

Scaling your database by driving conversions—both widespread and targeted—is important, but so is the ongoing engagement of those who have already converted. In Chapters Six and Seven, I discussed how content cadence plays just as important a role in category creation as content quality. An expectation gets set in the market that your brand is leading the conversation around industry best practices, along with a responsibility to deliver new and relevant content regularly into your marketable database. If contacts in your database are showing high engagement with the content that you're creating, that is a clear signal of their interest in your category. Signs of engagement for an already opted-in conversion can include interesting moments such as webinar attendance, regular visits to your blog or website, or registering to attend a live event. These moments impact that particular individual's behavioral data within the lead scoring component of your marketing automation system, which when correlated to demographic data, could be a good signal of "funnel two" interest in your products. We'll talk more about lead scoring from a category creation perspective later in this chapter.

It's worth measuring and communicating both conversions and ongoing marketing engagement through an account-based lens. While our focus in category creation must prioritize and empower people over logos, at the end of the day, companies in the B2B context enter into contractual agreements with other entities. Understanding how engaged contacts within your target accounts are with your content may signal where they are currently in their maturity within your category (funnel one) and whether or not they are in an active evaluation process for products (funnel two). Engagement with early stage content topics such as *how to build the team* may indicate they are still in strategy definition mode, while engagement with late stage content topics such as *how to use [your product] to solve X problem* may indicate they're in-market for a solution. Engagement can also correlate to how likely a forecasted deal is to close. If your sales team has deals in the forecast that haven't engaged with your website or content in some time, that opportunity may be at risk.

3. Pipeline Creation (Sourcing)

Conversions alone won't establish a category. Ultimately, you'll need to build the bridge from funnel one to funnel two by generating enough interest in your product to justify investments in category marketing. We'll spend a lot of time later in this chapter walking through some tactics to do just that, but the way to talk about converting category energy into product energy is in terms of MQLs, SQLs, and SALs. By implementing a lead scoring methodology, the conversions you've sourced at the top of the funnel are exhibiting demographic and behavioral context that can signal buying intent. Once they pass through a certain scoring threshold or exhibit behavior such as "hand raising" (asking for direct contact from sales), these conversions become MQLs that warrant a prospecting or qualification motion. The conversion-to-MQL conversion ratio is a good metric to observe for implied conversion from funnel one to funnel two.

What happens next is contextual to each company. In some organizations, MQLs generate alerts for the sales development team to follow up with in order to set a meeting for the account executive, and thus generating an SQL. Once the discovery call takes place, if the

AE believes the SDR correctly qualified the opportunity, they would *accept* the opportunity, thus creating an SAL. The rules of engagement, units of measurement, and compensation levers will differ from company to company. At the end of the day, these processes help mine category creation efforts for sales opportunities leveraging available data in marketing automation systems. Most marketing organizations are measured by pipeline creation, whether that shows up as MQLs, SQLs, or SALs. The trend, however, is to measure marketing further down the funnel, as pipeline created is only relevant if enough of it eventually turns into revenue. That's why sales and marketing alignment is absolutely critical to ensure that each organization is doing its part, especially in category creation where popular qualification methodologies like BANT (budget, authority, needs, and timeline) may not apply.

4. Pipeline Acceleration (Influence)

All individuals operating in a new category are in a constant state of learning, whether or not they are in-market for enabling products. In the previous scenarios, we discussed how category education efforts such as early stage content and event programs can generate interest in your brand, and when mined, can signal interest of buying intent. However, prospects who are already actively engaged in a sales process with your company also benefit from category education activities in profound ways. In fact, opportunities that are exhibiting increased levels of activity and engagement with your marketing programs have a higher propensity to buy. This means that when done right, marketing should influence nearly 100% of every deal closed in new categories, even if sourced by Sales, Customer Success, or other channels. Measuring influence and deal attribution is often a difficult (and contentious) exercise, but capturing interesting moments at an account level—as explored earlier in the database engagement section—is a great place to start. We'll cover some ideas later on how marketing can personalize thought leadership for sales to package at a specific account and, also, how late stage content can become a powerful lever to influence buyers in new categories and teach them how to buy.

5. New Business ARR

None of what I've shared in this book will matter unless the programs ultimately contribute to bookings—or a lead's successful journey through funnel two. The outcomes above are great leading indicators, but ARR (or revenue) is *the* lagging indicator of a category created. Typically, investors are interested in understanding how many new "lands"—or new logos—were closed in a given timeframe and, of those, how many transactions can be attributed to category marketing effort. To get ahead of that conversation, create a process around pulling together a detailed analysis of every deal closed, as well as conducting win (and even loss) interviews that capture qualitative feedback on why buyers buy. We've found time and time again in our customer interviews at Gainsight that customers loved our products, but when asked, it was our brand that compelled them to work with us over the competition.

6. Expansion ARR

Gainsight created an entire movement around the belief that closing a new deal is only the beginning of a brand's relationship with that customer. According to *Harvard Business Review*, the cost of acquiring a new customer is anywhere from five to 25 times more expensive than retaining an existing one.[2] Landing is clearly an important starting point, but Customer Success effort to help customers get value from

---

[2] Amy Gallo, "The Value of Keeping the Right Customers," *Harvard Business Review,* October 2014, https://hbr.org/2014/10/the-value-of-keeping-the-right -customers

the products we sell them generates powerful new revenue opportunities around (a) ensuring they renew their contracts, (b) upselling additional licenses or enhancements, or (c) cross-selling net new products. We'll talk about the value of category creation on customers in the final chapter of the book, but from the growth perspective, the same correlation of impact can be drawn to expansion revenue opportunities as new business opportunities. The financial KPI that CFOs and investors care about here may differ from company to company, but is typically net revenue retention (NRR). This metric measures the total value of your renewed contracts as well as the revenue gained through upsells and cross-sells. You can evaluate NRR on a monthly or annual basis, depending on your needs. Once you've determined the period of time you want to measure, add the value of your renewed contracts with your expansion revenue and divide it by the total value of all contracts that were up for renewal. Because upsells and cross-sells are taken into account, your NRR can be over 100%, and this is what best-in-class companies strive for.

There's another powerful way to connect category marketing effort to customer growth outside of the models described in the outcomes above—second order revenue. The idea is that the book has already been written on how to optimize sales and marketing spend as a function of customer lifetime value (CLTV). While imperfect, the calculation will typically be something to the tune of spending the first year's contract value (ACV) to acquire a new customer. But this calculation does not take into consideration virality and "second order" customers (as seen in Figure 12.1) that are sourced as opportunities when companies invest in Customer Success. Jason Lemkin, founder of SaaStr, illustrates a scenario[3] of second-order revenue as follows:

- At the end of Year 1, your champion quits Enterprise Customer A, but goes to Enterprise Customer B to do the exact same job. And buys your product again.

---

[3] Jason Lemkin, "CLTV Isn't the Whole Story. Don't Shortchange Second-Order Revenue," SaaStr, February 2013, https://www.saastr.com/its-not-just-cltv-its -your-trgcltv-that-matters-total-all-in-revenue-generated-by-your-customer/

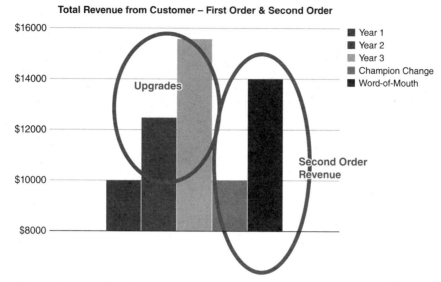

Figure 12.1 Visualizing the Effects of Second Order Revenue (via SaaStr)

- This happens about 10% of the time.
- So that first sale is actually worth $42,000 (the initial $38,000 deal x 110%).
- But then it happens again in Year 2. So it's really $46,000.
- And at the end of Year 1, your champion tells three of her friends about your company. And one of them purchases. About 30% of the time.
- So that first sale is actually worth $60,000, adding in the second order effects (viral, word-of-mouth, champion job changes, etc.)—*if* you make your customers super-duper happy.

Typically new markets will see a lot of executive turnover as demand for category experience and skill set outweighs supply. For category creators, that natural law creates an opportunity for champion change, repeat buyers, and viral word-of-mouth phenomena that creates second order pipeline creation—and therefore revenue. Making your customers successful is no longer just a

Figure 12.2   Charting Opportunity Cost in Conference Marketing

"post-sales" responsibility, but rather an important contributor to how revenue is generated.

Case Study on Growth: The Gainsight Pulse Conference

I hope by now you understand that category creation is directly correlated to growth. You won't need to invent any new metrics to convince your CFO or investors that these programs are working. But while results are typically measured using the point-in-time outcomes previously described, the reality is that executing the category creation playbook ends up feeling more like a perfect storm of activity and impact. One of the best examples of "success in chaos" is conference marketing, a strategy that I described in great detail in Chapter Eight. At Gainsight, as it is with every company that produces its own conference, the program impacts each of the growth outcomes described earlier in one powerful campaign. However, Pulse certainly comes at a price. Pulse represents Gainsight's single largest allocation of spend, so it's important that we seriously and objectively analyze each aspect of the conference with an eye toward optimization and evolution. After analyzing the data collected in the first five years of the conference (2013–2018), here's what we learned about Pulse's impact on Gainsight's growth.

- **Pulse Attendance Improves Close Rates.** Consistently, we see that Pulse has a huge upside to justify our investment (see Figure 12.2), both from net dollar burn and opportunity cost perspectives. Among opportunities existing for less than one year prior to Pulse 2016, Gainsight had 3.5x higher likelihood of closing the deal with Pulse attendees; those who took meetings with our sales team onsite closed at more than 4.5x higher rate. While the Pulse experience may lead to higher conversions, we could also conclude that non-attendance expresses a lack of interest and lower likelihood of purchase. In other words, Pulse non-attendance may be an indicator of prospect health. Accordingly, we dedicate fewer sales resources to non-attendees.
- **Pulse Attendance Drives Higher Average Contract Values (ACVs).** Also among these existing opportunities, we are seeing higher ASPs—more than 40% higher for attendees and another 10 points for those with meetings (see Figure 12.3). Notably, this trend is consistent across segments and not just because enterprise deals are those with Pulse attendance.
- **Pulse Attendance Drives Higher Logo Retention.** We also closely examined the relationship between attendance and retention. When looking at churned customers (see Figure 12.4), their attendance rates are lower. We've seen that customers with employees attending have 13 points higher logo retention and 41 points higher net retention; those with meetings retain at even higher rates. Though customer attendance may indeed drive Gainsight adoption, non-attendance (just as with prospects) could suggest a lack of interest in Gainsight and Customer Success. Simply put, Pulse non-attendance may be an indicator of customer health.

We've concluded over the years that, hands down, Pulse is the single most important program that Gainsight runs—in terms of expanding the total addressable market (TAM) of the category, driving the growth of the company, as well as advancing the company's relationship and leadership equity with customers, investors, and employees. Our strategy over time is to keep scaling the growth of the conference and the experience we create for attendees, while

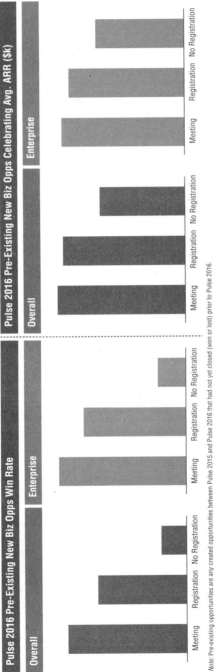

Note: Pre-existing opportunities are any created opportunities between Pulse 2015 and Pulse 2016 that had not yet closed (won or lost) prior to Pulse 2016.

Figure 12.3 Understanding ACV Impact of Pulse Conference Attendance

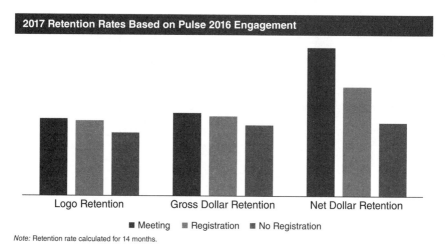

2017 Retention Rates Based on Pulse 2016 Engagement

Logo Retention　　　Gross Dollar Retention　　　Net Dollar Retention

■ Meeting　■ Registration　■ No Registration

Note: Retention rate calculated for 14 months.

Figure 12.4　Understanding Retention Impact of Pulse Conference Attendance

also driving down our operational costs on the program. Both economies of scale (registration revenue) and a growing partner ecosystem (sponsor revenue) help in that effort.

How to Build a Bridge into Funnel Two

Successfully building a bridge from category interest (funnel one) to product interest (funnel two) is the single biggest challenge in category creation. It's entirely possible the conversions are spiking and interest in the category is extremely high, and yet, Sales is still forecasting below plan. The primary reason for this phenomenon comes back to education—with the exception of early adopters, the market at large will typically need to define strategy prior to taking a chance at a product to operationalize that very strategy. That process takes time, and category creators play an important role in serving the market as thought partners throughout that phase of the journey. This chasm will manifest to executives and investors in a few ways, but most interesting is in opportunity loss reasons, which in new

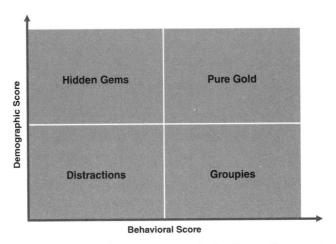

Figure 12.5   Lead Scoring Framework for New Categories

categories typically tend not to be losses to competition, but rather, losses to time (or not now). Prospects in funnel one are learning how to solve the problem that you've observed in the category—a process that for some companies could take a long time. How can you short-circuit the new category learning curve?

The first step is to understand how to prioritize marketing programs in context of those companies that are showing signals of interest in funnel two, over companies that are very happy living in funnel one. Time is an important currency in business, so aligning marketing and sales resources against accounts with the highest propensity to buy now is important. To understand what's going on in your marketable database, you need to implement a lead scoring methodology. Lead scores are assigned to each contact in your database and measure important factors such as demographic data (e.g., Is this the right type of company, or are they a buyer or influencer persona?) and behavioral data (e.g., How often is this contact on our website, or has she registered for an event recently?). As the contact engages with your brand through various programs, his or her behavioral score improves, which can indicate intention and prioritize action for sales and marketing. By passing a certain scoring threshold, that contact becomes an MQL. Figure 12.5 introduces a framework for thinking about lead scoring in context of category creation. The idea is that each contact in your database can be organized into four buckets, indicating where the contact is in the journey with your brand.

The idea is that contacts receive a demographic score when they enter your database initially as a conversion. A buyer or influencer from a target account, for example, would likely rank in the upper quartile of the vertical axis, rather than an individual contributor from a vertical outside of your core market in the lower quartile. Once someone becomes a conversion, her ongoing engagement with your brand will move the behavioral score left and right on the horizontal axis, with an arbitrary threshold in the middle that separates the two columns. Here's how the different cohorts break down in order of priority:

- **Pure Gold.** Highly qualified, highly engaged. These are contacts who should be paying customers of your product and have leaned into your thought leadership. Fast-track these leads to ensure you're deploying a high-touch nurture effort, or that Sales is engaged in a qualification effort.
- **Hidden Gems.** Highly qualified, low engagement. These are also contacts who should become paying customers, but are not showing obvious signals of engagement with your brand. This is the next logical space to spend your prospecting efforts, typically by enrolling these contacts into a high-touch nurture effort designed to improve their behavior scores.
- **Groupies.** Not qualified, but high engagement. Groupies are critically important to building your category (funnel one), but may prove to be red herrings for product sales. They'll retweet everything you post, come to every conference and webinar, but more than likely, will never buy anything from you. It's important not to dismiss groupies (since they are valued members of the community you are building), but your sales and marketing efforts may yield better results focused on contacts in the former two buckets.
- **Distractions.** Not qualified, low engagement. Don't waste too much of your effort trying to monetize contacts in this bucket. Like "Groupies," however, it's important to keep an eye

on this cohort as community members and brand advocates—
especially as their behavioral score improves over time.

Once you've made sense of your database, you are now ready to
run programs to uncover buying intent for your product. Even the
most engaged contacts (Pure Golds and Groupies) can appear to have
bought into your value proposition, but are not actually empowered
to buy product. You've won their hearts, but you won't be successful
in bridging to funnel two until you've won their minds. Here are
some of the hacks you can deploy to aid in that effort:

- **Position Your Solution as a Painkiller, Not a Vitamin.** It's
  difficult to create urgency around selling products if they are perceived as a "nice to have" or not mission-critical to success in your
  category. That's where messaging comes in, but crafting language
  around a burning reason to buy now is impossible without compelling data that can justify the expense. Consider conducting an
  ROI research project in order to determine the value drivers of
  investment in your category and, also, the incremental value created by investment in your product. I gave an in-depth example
  of an ROI project we conducted early at Gainsight in Chapter
  Three. The outcomes of this project are important data points
  that can be promoted in messaging on the website or in sales
  decks, but also a longer-form content asset that can enable your
  champions at the prospect company to justify an investment in
  (or at least evaluation of) your product. Data can inspire action,
  and when promoted the right way, create a sense of FOMO (fear
  of missing out) among individuals in new markets.
- **Teach Them How to Buy.** Recall that in new categories,
  chances are that your audience has never bought a product
  to solve this particular problem before (otherwise, is it *really* a
  new category?). Once approved to start a product evaluation,
  prospects may not understand how to define their selection
  criteria or what a typical sales process looks like. Category creators see this as an opportunity to engineer the sales process
  for their category and to teach the market *how* to buy products. Create the official "buyers guide" content asset for your

category that educates the market on important considerations for evaluating solutions. Draft a sample RFP document that provides a checklist of features and benefits that the market can use in vendor selection. Maintain integrity in how that content is produced, but ensure that the value of your product is well positioned. This effort is quite literally constructing the bridge from funnel one to funnel two and putting your sales team in a position to create repeatable motions for monetizing category thought leadership.

- **Let Your Customers Do the Talking.** Telling the world you have the number 1 product in your category is good, but creating a platform for your customers to express that same position is a much more effective approach. The customer marketing programs we reviewed in Chapter Nine such as case studies and testimonial videos capture customer stories and validate a prospect's journey from the first to second funnel. Herd mentality is a very real part of the modern sales motion, as prospects can be influenced by their peers to consider new products on a largely emotional, rather than rational, basis. Leveraging the endorsement of happy and successful customers will build confidence in your young market and accelerate sales velocity.

These hacks are characterized as "late stage" content assets and campaigns, which, as I described in Chapter Six, are typically either locked behind a gate or in a content management system for the sales team to use in deal cycles. In order to build the bridge into funnel two, category creators need to create widespread awareness and urgency around their product value by promoting these assets at the very top of the funnel. Social, blog posts, email—these evangelism channels are typically reserved for early stage content about the category (and not your products), but are appropriate channels to win the minds of your market and enable them to self-actualize in your category to an even greater degree through the use of your products and services. As they engage with late stage content, make sure to apply the appropriate weighting to those moments, as they are even stronger indicators of buying interest than early stage signals.

Category creation programs drive growth—but the truth is that each market will have its own nuance. Use the tools presented in this chapter as a means of measuring the success of your programs and communicating the impact of your efforts on growth, but a spirit of humility will serve you well on your journey. Marketers will benefit from taking a servant leadership position with their Sales counterparts—anticipating their needs and putting their sellers in a position to win. Sales will benefit from sharing their learning with Marketing. But these two constituencies are only two of the many actors who contribute to, and benefit from, category creation—and as Einstein said, "Not everything that counts can be counted." Our final chapter will explore the intangible benefits of category creation, particularly the impact on its most important benefactors—customers and teammates.

13 | The Intangible Benefits of Category Creation on Customer and Teammate Success

If I could trade *marketing* careers with anyone in the world, it would be with a man named Duncan Wardle. Duncan's business card is surely the envy of any marketer who has ever preferred right-brain strategy over left—he was the former vice president of innovation and creativity at The Walt Disney Company. Over his 25-year career at Disney, Duncan was responsible for developing some of the company's most innovative ideas and strategies, including sending a Buzz Lightyear action figure to (literal) outer space on NASA's Space Shuttle Discovery to promote the launch of a new attraction at Walt Disney World. Today, Duncan is on the road speaking at events, leading workshops, and hosting ideation sessions at customer sites. His mission? To challenge *everyone* to claim his or her own creativity, and thus create a culture of innovation never possible before.

One of the ways that companies can create that culture is to realize that, as Duncan puts it, "People are not buying products and services anymore, they are buying purpose. And in order for them to understand your purpose they must understand your story." That's a deeply profound statement, and one that is especially true for category creators. I discussed in Chapter Five the importance of articulating and expressing company purpose—in fact, it's the foundational step of the category creation playbook. Tell your story the right way, and there are transformative implications to be realized on two of the most important constituencies within your category:

1. Customers, who want to do business with purpose-driven companies.
2. Teammates, who want to contribute to the mission of purpose-driven companies.

Customers, especially the early adopters in new categories, are entering into commercial agreements with your business because they buy into your purpose—your products and services just happen to be a (critical) part of that expression. Other components of that decision-making framework, on equal or greater footing with the actual product, include the content and event programs you develop to help your customers reach their fullest potential, the experience that you and your team create across the customer lifecycle, and any other expression of purpose that serves the people in the market you are creating. The outcomes, at least the tangible ones, can show up in lagging indicators such as net promoter score (NPS) surveys that measure customer happiness, renewals or retention rates that measure customer loyalty, or expansion revenue (as discussed in Chapter Twelve) that measures customer growth.

Teammates, perhaps as internal customers of the brand, buy into purpose from the moment they sign their offer letters and throughout their journey as employees of your organization. Professionals in today's economy have more options than ever before of companies they can choose to work for, and the so-called "talent wars" have placed a critical emphasis on keeping employees engaged and fulfilled. In a recent study by Culture Amp, the Culture First employee feedback company, the company proved a correlation of share price growth to employee

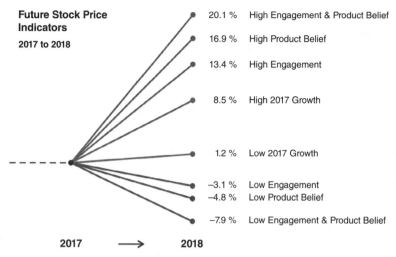

Figure 13.1   Future Stock Price Indicators of Employee Engagement and Product Belief

feedback data from over 70 publicly listed companies. They found that employee perceptions are strong leading indicators of important future outcomes. As the chart in Figure 13.1 illustrates, higher employee engagement in 2017 was associated with 16.5% higher share price growth YTD 2018.[1] Combine that effect with product belief, and the association grew to 27.9% higher YTD growth. The takeaways are clear—creating a culture that keeps teammates engaged on the journey to purpose realization impacts so much more than happiness and loyalty (although those are important), but a company's financial outcomes as well.

These quantifiable measures of impact can be true for any purpose-driven organization, but are especially true for category creators. The whole notion of creating a new market category implies a noble endeavor in and of itself, and solving a complex problem that people don't know they have requires deep conviction and courage. But the journey also reveals a set of *intangible* benefits for customers and teammates who are enrolled in the mission, aligning hearts and minds

---

[1] Jason McPherson, "The ROI of Employee Engagement and Culture," Culture Amp, https://blog.cultureamp.com/the-roi-of-employee-engagement-and-culture

behind a movement in the marketplace led by an inspiring and category-defining brand. Let's unpack some of those intangible benefits here:

- **Radically High Ambition.** It's hard enough to find a wave to surf to shore, let alone to create a net new wave. The truth is that every industry is chock-full of examples of companies that have identified market trends and successfully executed against those opportunities. Some of those disruptor businesses may have experienced a lot of success, perhaps by delivering incredible product experiences, without the need to create a new category—companies like Slack and Zoom come to mind as examples. However, while it matters that category creators can out-surf the competition, harnessing the energy to generate new waves as well takes a radical sense of ambition that is extremely attractive to the right set of customers and teammates. In Chapter Six, I explained that early adopters will not only buy into your company's bold purpose, but they'll also root for your success along the way. Ambition is inspiring and can almost create a kinetic energy around your brand that draws customers in and keeps them engaged. Employees too are drawn toward opportunities to create their best work, develop professionally, and perform at a very high level. Admittedly, career opportunities at category creators may not be for everyone—but those who are inspired by the hard thing about hard things will align their personal sense of purpose and high ambition with that of the company.

- **People Centricity.** Chapter Six also revealed that at the heart of new categories are people, humans who identify and resonate deeply with the noble mission and purpose your company endeavors to fulfill. While illustrations of our future existence are characterized by a *Blade Runner*–esque dystopian outlook where AI and automation make human progress irrelevant, category creation seeks to make a case for a future where humans come first. For many customers and teammates who place an emphasis on community within their personal and professional lives, that's a reality worth fighting for. This is an especially important point in industries like software, where finding deep meaning in work is often more difficult than, say, in the life sciences. By aligning personal purpose to building technology in the service of people, the right customers and teammates will become faithful participants in the category's mission. Also, the relationships developed within the community itself are much deeper and less transactional than typical vendor/customer/partner interaction within product-centric industries. Personally, I've had the privilege of observing meaningful relationships form in the Customer Success community that span across geography and job title—the common denominator being people helping people as they look to define strategy, build teams, or find new career opportunities. What an awesome opportunity for category creators to serve as stewards of that platform.

- **Pioneering Spirit.** It takes a special type of person to desire going where no one has gone before, especially in markets where easier opportunities may be available. This entrepreneurial or intrapreneurial spirit is prevalent in every facet of new markets, whether in customers looking to bring new strategies into their businesses for the very first time or teammates at all levels of the organization bringing a beginner's mind into their work every single day. Category creation means writing the pages of the history book for a brand new industry—a process that invites unprecedented levels of transparency and cross-departmental (and organizational) collaboration in order to recognize the patterns of what will work in context of the specific market. Getting comfortable with transparency can often be a difficult thing for some, but the rewards both personally and professionally for those within the company and community who do will pay dividends throughout their careers.

While (again) category creation is not for everyone, the benefits both tangible and intangible for customers and teammates alike are enough to attract, engage, and develop the right individuals who identify with the purpose of the company on top. Beyond those constituents, partners will also be interested in aligning with category leaders to share in the thought leadership energy being created with hopes of their paths to monetization.

For integration partners, this could benefit your company by extending product functionality and capability to address emerging use cases within the category, while also co-marketing with the partner in order to share leads and build influence.

For systems integrators and large consultancies, partners may be interested in building a practice within the new category, desiring a piece of your thought leadership in exchange for product referrals. In most cases, these partners are looking to sell services oriented around a business transformation project at large companies—ideally, with your product as the operational element within that transaction.

For private equity or venture capital partners, developing a "friends-and-family" package that can be promoted to portfolio companies could drive lead volume, while also creating value for the firm itself. These opportunities (and others) can help fuel category momentum, while also delivering benefit for company, partner, and customer.

Spotlight on Sales Teams

There's one team in particular that may require additional perspective for category creation—the sales organization. Depending on the sales leadership you recruit, sales processes you install, the culture you create, and the rep profile you develop, the long-term greed required for success in new categories will be met with different reactions.

One profile of sales professional is extremely goal-oriented around making money—driven by the wealth creation potential of a successful career in the discipline. There's no judgment whatsoever around that mindset, as the only person within any business who should be compensated as much, if not more than your CEO is your top performing sales rep. But great salespeople are constantly being recruited by companies, many of which have found product-market fit in an established category and are in "land grab" mode. For these types of opportunities, the business is not lead or opportunity constrained, but, if anything, is time or capacity constrained and needs to ramp sales hiring to fulfill its ambition. The compelling recruitment message to this type of rep profile is quite simple—come on board, hit your numbers, and you'll make a lot of money.

While having some of this sales DNA within an organization creating a category is not necessarily bad, it could present some performance or even attrition risk for those who haven't bought into the mission. As companies evolve through various stages of category maturity, it's entirely possible that the risk diminishes as repeatable sales motions are established and high-performing reps have modeled success for the organization.

However, there's one profile of sales professional that thrives in the category creation environment—*value sellers*. Value selling is a sales methodology that advocates for understanding and reinforcing the reason why your offer is valuable to the purchaser. The idea is to always sell based on the value your offer provides, not the cost. We know that in modern business, your offer is so much more than just the products you sell (thank you, Duncan Wardle)—so packaging the entire brand value proposition (your content, community, and expertise) will resonate deeply with executive buyers who are looking to drive outcomes, not buy products. Juxtapose that selling motion against commoditized products (think online storage as an example) where companies can often compete on price. Put simply, category creation can make life a lot easier for value sellers, who in turn can create massive impact for the company while creating some personal wealth of their own along the way.

The Alliance of Working and Winning in Category Creation

There's a phenomenal book on talent management written by Reid Hoffman, Ben Casnocha, and Chris Yeh called *The Alliance: Managing Talent in the Networked Age*. The reason these authors wrote the book, all well-esteemed entrepreneurs and investors in their own rights, was based on a belief that the employer-employee relationship is fundamentally broken and the old model of guaranteeing long-term employment no longer works in a business environment that's defined by continuous change. The solution they propose is to stop thinking of employees as either family or free agents, but instead as allies with whom alliances can be formed. Companies are looking for business transformation and impact from their employees, while the employees themselves are interested in career transformation in return. Within the context of that alliance, companies can maintain trust with their employees, while also recruiting and retaining entrepreneurial talent to adapt to business needs as they evolve over time.

The Alliance is an especially important philosophy to embed into the talent management strategy for category creators. The spirit of this was inspired by a recent tweet from my CEO, Nick Mehta (see Figure 13.2). The reality is that companies in new categories evolve through many generations as they go down the long road of building something new. As I described earlier, the opportunity to be part of a category creation story is an extremely attractive offer for the right type of talent, but even the most engaged employees will eventually leave. It's easy as a CEO to carry the weight of that pressure on your shoulders, but adopting the principles of *The Alliance* and seeing the

Figure 13.2 Tweet from Gainsight CEO Nick Mehta

humanity of the team (as Nick states) can help rationalize what is otherwise a very emotional concept.

Thinking about the humanity of our teammates means realizing that while everyone is invested in the success of the company and category, the extent of that investment is different for each individual. For some, there's a financial outcome on the other end of that success—whether cash or stock compensation—which can influence performance and retention. For others, being associated with a category creator is motivation enough and can serve as the golden chapter in the story arc of their careers. Understanding that humanity and operationalizing a talent management strategy that builds on those motivators can be a powerful mechanism to engage teammates and prepare them for a life after the company they're helping to create. Imagine launching a learning development initiative, as an example, that invests in the education and professional growth of the team— building skills that can be applied on the job while also activating passions and curiosity outside of their functional domain. Programs like these can make working for your company so much more than "just a job" and contribute impactfully to keeping employees engaged and retained for the long road ahead.

But ultimately, you can't be proactive with a human-first talent management strategy unless you are winning in business. Success is the ultimate engagement and retention strategy, as teammates are quite literally betting their careers on companies that are selling them on potential. Of course, success at all costs is not the lesson here, but as companies hit their numbers, improve financial metrics, and deliver an incredible product experience, these wins reassure teammates that they've chosen the right brand and can shine a light on the personal impact of their efforts on company performance. In the category creation context, this means not just creating the category, but hitting the right milestones along the journey that signal the category domination strategy is indeed working. The specific definition of winning may be different in each industry, but it's consistent for any company whether or not they're creating or disrupting a market.

This revelation leads to a discussion on the other side of *The Alliance* framework: What do category creators require of employees in order to win in business and, therefore, deliver on their teammate value proposition? Delivering the outcomes that they are measured by may be the obvious answer, but in fact, metrics alone are not enough. This is especially important as companies mature and become increasingly siloed—for example, imagine a case where Marketing hits their metrics as leading indicators of sales, but that effort does not show up as bookings in ARR. Never happens, right? To help drive collaboration and engagement across departments and create a spirit where **everyone** within the organization can help the company win, here are several *intangible* aspects of a healthy alliance that companies should consider promoting to their teams:

- **Transparency.** Creating a culture of winning together requires open dialogue on what each individual at the company is learning along the journey. Teammates should feel comfortable sharing both success and failures without fear of reprimand or judgment. While this book shares a lot of the lessons learned from category creation, the truth is that a lot of the lessons will have to be learned by you and your teams. The best of breed companies embrace transparency and use internal communication processes to share learning that can influence decisions across the organization.
- **Buy-In.** The moment that a teammate loses faith in the company, strategy, management, or mission, he's out of the game. Buy-in starts with a fundamental belief in the strategy that the leadership team sets forth and that each individual's work is meaningful and contributes to company goals. If there's a component of strategy that was missed or overlooked, companies need their employees to engage and bring that to light. But since companies are made up of individuals, it's unlikely that every individual will agree to each aspect of company strategy. That's where the management principle of *disagree and commit* can be helpful, a doctrine which states that individuals are allowed to disagree while a decision is being made, but that once a decision has been made, everybody must commit to it.

- **Candor.** Since category creation by its nature will require both learning and adaptability, it's important that teammates share their feedback, creative ideas, and roadblocks with the broader team. Kim Scott's bestselling book *Radical Candor: Be a Kick-Ass Boss Without Losing Your Humanity* says it best, that challenging people is often the best way to show you care. It does not mean that whatever you think is the truth; it means you share your (humble) opinions directly.
- **Rigor.** Stay long-term greedy. Companies need teammates to stay hungry and find ways to activate their ambition as the category and company are being developed. It's easy for teammates to lose focus or, in some cases, to look for ambition outside the walls of the company. The journey is lumpy and will almost certainly include both highs and lows. Sometimes finding a way to simply stay in the game is enough motivation to ride out the lows and spark that fire all over again. Category creation *requires* passion and energy within the team in order to will a new market into existence—there's no place for apathy in this model.

Conclusion

There's arguably been no other business strategy in modern times that's been shrouded in mystery and intrigue quite like category creation. Sure, everyone wants to be a category creator, but understanding *how* to do it and knowing that it's working can often stop an entrepreneur or executive right in her tracks. That's exactly why I decided to write this book—not to provide rose-tinted glasses on how category creation is an easy strategy that every business should deploy. Long-term greed is foundational—if there were an easier path to building a market, then that disclosure may not have been a necessary reiteration throughout the text.

But if you're still reading this and, after all my words of warning, still believe that you and your team have the courage to create a market around a problem that people may have felt but have never before articulated—then welcome to the club. You'll find great reward and fulfillment on the other end of your journey—for yourself, your customers, investors, and teammates. While this book may be printed and published, the reality is that there will be many revisions in time as we grow and learn together as a community of creators. Don't lose that courage, and remember, most importantly, you are no longer alone.

Acknowledgments

I want to start by giving thanks to the ultimate Creator, who has blessed me abundantly with relationships and opportunities that have profoundly shaped my life and career. Through His Son, He has given every aspect of my life an eternal perspective—yes, even enterprise software. All glory to God for the opportunity to write this story.

Thank you to my beautiful and encouraging wife Brittany, who always told me that I was a good writer (will let the court of public opinion now decide if she's right). I wrote *Category Creation* over a two-and-a-half-month window of time that happened to overlap with (a) months eight to ten of our young daughter's life, (b) preparation and presentation of Brittany's master's thesis, and (c) planning a 5,500+ person conference at Moscone Center. We were constantly stressed, usually sleep deprived, and each working independently toward our dreams. Brittany sacrificed the most—ensuring that she never skipped a beat as an incredible and intentional mother while successfully defending her thesis. She's my superhero, and I'm thankful every day that she agreed to be on this crazy journey called life with me.

I am so grateful for my lovely daughter Cienna Brielle, whose hallway smiles and occasional office distractions fueled my motivation to get the book published and make her proud of her daddy. My wish for her is to reach her fullest potential in *every* aspect of life, and that through my efforts both at work and at home, I can play my small part in creating a more inclusive world where she has the same opportunities to pursue her dreams and passions that I have had in my life.

I want to thank my entire family for their encouragement and patience during the long nights and weekends of writing—especially my beautiful mom Rita, Brittany's parents Mark and Cindy, my dad Mike, Karin and Kailyn, my uncle Rody, Bill and Carole, Tiffany and Justin, Brian, Melissa and Eric, and everyone else. While I tried my best to be present with the family during this intense season of life, I know that I often fell short. Thank you for loving me anyway.

There would be no *Category Creation* without Nick Mehta, who took a chance on a 26-year-old punk from Los Angeles to build Gainsight with from the ground up. The ideas that inspired the plays now memorialized in this book did not come in isolation, but through inspiring brainstorms with Nick and others. Not every idea worked (perhaps we'll reserve those for the sequel), but many did, and together, we were able to inspire an entire community to win in business while being human first. Nick is well respected across the industry for his values-based and people-centric leadership, but not much (yet) is written on the tailwind he creates for his team to chase big ideas. His encouragement and sponsorship made this book a reality, and I can only hope to make him proud by reflecting even a glimmer of his greatness at Gainsight and beyond.

A huge thank you to the entire Gainsight marketing team for letting me tell your story—especially in the months building to the biggest (and most complex) Pulse conference we've ever done. You are the co-authors of this book, the category creators behind Customer Success, who have forever changed how companies market, sell, and serve their customers in the business-to-human (B2H) world. A special thank you to my direct reports, who carried a lot of the workload while I moonlit on this project, including Lauren Olerich, Lauren Sommers, Mike Berger, Mike Manheimer, and Scott Salkin. You've put up with a lot of crazy ideas from me over the years, but you are the imagineers who made those dreams come to life. #OneTeam

Thank you to the incredible team at Wiley for giving this first-time author the opportunity to publish a book into the mainstream business audience—especially Richard Narramore, Victoria Anllo, and Vicki Adang. In an increasingly digital world, category creation best practices may be discovered decentralized and scattered in blog posts and videos across the Internet. With your support, now entrepreneurs and executives across the world can learn from our mistakes and create sustainable value in the global economy by inventing new markets of products and services of their own.

A huge thank you to those who contributed their voices to *Category Creation* by writing pages of the playbook—you are category creators who inspire me, and I'm humbled that you were willing to take time out of your busy schedule to be a part of this. I especially want to thank Brian Halligan and Andrew Mahon at HubSpot—I salute you with a *Wayne's World*, "I am not worthy!" bow for writing the foreword. The HubSpot story of creating the Inbound Marketing category inspired a lot of what we built at Gainsight, and having your endorsement on the playbook is a lifetime achievement for me. I also want to thank Maria Pergolino, Mark Organ, and Mike Fauscette for their contributions. I've learned so much from each of you over the years, and the opportunity to turn the mic to you is an honor that I'll cherish forever. There were several other innovators I referenced throughout the book who have inspired a lot of my thinking over the years—especially Dan Rogers, David Gerhardt, Jason Lemkin, John Rex, Kaley Klemp, Keith Krach, Marc Benioff, and Max Altschuler.

The intent behind writing *Category Creation* was never to sell more licenses of Gainsight software—if so, we probably would have written something that targeted the Customer Success audience rather than entrepreneurs, GTM executives, and marketers. This book was written as a passion project, pouring out of the hearts and minds of the innovators named here who have learned an enormous amount about this emerging business practice and want to pay it forward to those who come next. So thank you to YOU, the reader, for supporting this movement and pursuing original ideas and the road less traveled to will them into reality. Stay hungry, stay foolish. Mamba out.

Index

Note: Page references in *italics* refer to figures.